M. L Hawley

The Psalms in Meter

M. L Hawley
The Psalms in Meter
ISBN/EAN: 9783744783774
Printed in Europe, USA, Canada, Australia, Japan
Cover: Foto ©Lupo / pixelio.de

More available books at **www.hansebooks.com**

THE

PSALMS IN METER.

By Rev. M. L. HAWLEY,
OF THE BALTIMORE CONFERENCE, M. E. CHURCH.

———◆———

PUBLISHED FOR THE AUTHOR.
CARLTON & LANAHAN,
200 MULBERRY-STREET, N. Y.
1868.

Entered according to Act of Congress, in the year 1868, by

M. L. HAWLEY,

in the Clerk's Office of the District Court of the United States for the Southern District of New York.

PREFACE.

I was gradually led to undertake this work. The First Psalm was written without intention to proceed further. Then a number of other Psalms were selected on which to bestow similar labor. But this labor disclosed to my mind beauty, sublimity, and bold poetic imagery in the Psalms which it had hitherto overlooked. Then the versification of all the Psalms was conceived, and it was, as rapidly as circumstances allowed, carried to a completion.

It was at first my intention to prepare a volume of Lyrics suitable to be sung in the Christian Church. And, indeed, this intention was kept prominently in view to the last, although it was soon found that many of the Psalms are wholly unsuitable for such use. These Psalms are changed into easy and, in some instances, careless measure and rhyme. And others, doubtless, would have better expressed the mind of the sacred writers if attempt had not been made to change them to Christian Lyrics. The whole might properly be divided into three classes: Psalms for Public Worship, Psalms for Private Devotion, and Psalms for Ordinary Reading.

In this versification a Psalm was not merely selected as the foundation of a hymn, rejecting sentiments of the sacred writer, and adding thoughts of the versifier, as did a distinguished English Lyrist; but the attempt was made to give most of the Psalms entire and pure, without abbreviation, and without addition. The abbreviations which occur are not of sentiments, but of repetitions; for in Hebrew poetry, by a peculiarity known as *parallelism*, the same thought, with slight variations, is frequently several times repeated. And the additions, which are few, either are implied in the Psalms, or serve to explain and enforce the sentiments of the sacred writers. These compositions are properly paraphrases.

In attempting to change the Psalms to Christian Lyrics, it was frequently necessary to substitute the appellation Christ for that of Lord or Jehovah. But this is perfectly admissible, as Christ is acknowledged to be the Jehovah of the Old Testament. It was also necessary

PREFACE. 5

to give Psalms of a secular character a spiritual or religious application. The Forty-fifth Psalm may be particularly mentioned. But this is justifiable according to the allegorical method of interpretation.

The question naturally arises here, Do any of the Psalms relate to Christ? Some modern critics are disposed to answer negatively. They claim that the writers of the Psalms make no allusion to the Messiah, and that Christ and the apostles argue "*ex concessis*," that is, from the acknowledged opinion of their opponents or contemporaries, without vouching for their correctness when they give any of the Psalms such an application. This position is to be deplored; for even if true it is not the whole truth, and is calculated to weaken confidence in the Scriptures, and in the Saviour they describe. That in the minds of the writers of the Psalms there was no reference to the Messiah may be safely admitted; but that there was no such reference in the Divine Mind is certainly untrue. Under the influence of Divine inspiration the sacred writers frequently wrote what they did not fully understand; and though the Psalmists may not have had Christ in view, they actually wrote of him. And every passage of Scripture which the New Testament writers apply to Christ, doubtless, in the Divine Mind had such an application. Besides, to argue as claimed in this position was not simply to perplex, but to deceive. Surely no Christian writer will defend a position which involves such a conclusion. And our Lord positively claims that he is the subject of prediction in the Psalms. "All things must be fulfilled which are written in the law of Moses, and in the prophets, and in the PSALMS concerning me." Luke xxiv, 44.

It may be well here to express an opinion respecting the imprecations or maledictions contained in some of the Psalms. Writers are accustomed to admit that they are not in harmony with the teachings of the Gospel, nor even with the spirit of the religion of the Jews. But they plead in palliation that prayer for the destruction of foes is equivalent to prayer for personal deliverance and preservation. But are not these imprecations the utterances of indignation rather than of malice? Are they not prayers based upon desire for the destruction of sin rather than of sinners? They contain no evidence of vindictive feeling toward the wicked. And we should also recollect that the language of emotion does not always admit of a literal interpretation.

The division of the Psalms into books is at least as old as the Septuagint version. These books were doubtless collected by different persons, and at different periods. This accounts for the identity of the Fourteenth and Fifty-third Psalms, and of fragments of some of the other Psalms. The compiler of the third division, in which there are none of the Psalms of David, probably added the note at the end of the second book, "Here end the Psalms of David, the son of Jesse." David, however, is the author of several Psalms in the two succeeding books.

In the composition of this work, it was found exceedingly difficult to change the Psalms to even tolerable English poetry. Frequently a far happier turn of thought presented itself; but the sentiments of another had to be expressed, and it was consequently rejected. The labor was much like that of writing an acrostic, restrained, without the mental freedom needed especially by the poet. But only the One Hundred and Thirty-ninth Psalm caused any misgiving in attempting a versification. Its sentiments are so sacred and elevated, and its diction is so bold and sublime, that attempt to versify it seemed rashness; and for some time the thought was seriously entertained of transferring it to this volume, without attempting to reduce it to measure and rhyme. And now, in submitting "The Psalms in Meter" to the public, it is desired the work should be judged in view of the intention of the author to produce a metrical translation, rather than a paraphrase, of the Psalms; and by comparison with similar productions by others, rather than upon its own intrinsic merits.

August 29, 1868.

THE
PSALMS IN METER.

BOOK I.

PSALM I.

The Righteous and the Wicked contrasted.

BLESSED is the man who shuns the path
   Trod by unholy feet,
Who stands not in the sinner's way,
   Nor takes the scoffer's seat;
But meditates, with pure delight,
On God's just law both day and night.

He's like the tree beside a stream,
   That yields a pleasant shade;
Its fruit maturing at its time,
   Its leaves not known to fade:
And should change come, secure is he—
His lot in life, prosperity.

Not so the wicked in their state;
   How insecure are they!

At best they are like worthless chaff
　　The wind drives swift away:
They shall not with the righteous stand
When angry judgments sweep the land.

God knows the way the just pursue;
　　And he will surely bless,
And guard from every enemy,
　　Their works of righteousness;
But he the wicked will assail,
And every sinful way shall fail.

PSALM II.

Triumph of Christ over his Foes.

WHY do the heathen nations rage,
　　And things impossible design?
Why 'gainst Jehovah and his Christ
　　Earth's mighty ones combine?
"Come, let us break their bonds," they say,
"And let us cast their cords away."

The Lord, who ever reigns supreme,
　　Will their vain thoughts and aims deride;
Yea, he will in displeasure speak,
　　And utterly confound their pride:
"I have my Son placed on the throne,
And him shall all the nations own."

Now hear what God to me has said:
  "Thou art my own Eternal Son;
Ask, and the people shall be thine—
  The world to thy just cause be won:
For strong thou shalt thy scepter make,
And foes as a frail vessel break."

Hence, mighty ones in crime, be wise;
  Heed well the admonition given;
With awe obey, with fear adore
  The Lord, who rules in earth and heaven:
The favor of the Son make sure,
For blessed are they in him secure.

PSALM III.

The Confidence of the Righteous.

MY foes, O Lord, increase each day;
  They come against me as a flood;
And with relentless hatred say,
  "There is no help for him in God:"
But Thou, my glory, shield, and hope,
Liftest my head in safety up.

To thee I cried, O God most pure,
  Who deignedst ardent prayer to hear;
Then laid me down and slept secure,
  For my Preserver still was near:

And I need suffer no alarm,
Though thousands join to do me harm.

The wicked thou hast smitten down,
    And dealt my foes a fatal blow;
And now, O Lord, thy mercies crown,
    And let me all thy goodness know:
For power to save to thee belongs,
And thy rich blessings claim our songs.

PSALM IV.

Evening Prayer.

O GOD, thou art my righteousness;
    Bend to my cry thine ear;
Oft thou hast helped me in distress—
    Again in mercy hear.

How long will men despise the just?
    Love vanity and lies?
God them exalts who in him trust,
    And hears their earnest cries.

Then stand in awe, and sin avoid;
    Reflect in night's lone hour;
Offer oblations to the Lord,
    And trust his saving power.

Yet many say, "There is no hope;
    Who us will favor show?"

Thy smile, O Lord, on us lift up;
  Let us thy goodness know.

Their joys when corn and wine increase,
  My gladness doth excel;
For watched by thee I sleep in peace,
  In perfect safety dwell.

PSALM V.

Morning Prayer.

HEAR my words, O gracious Saviour,
  Listen to my earnest cry;
Turn not from my supplication,
  For to thee I lift mine eye.

Thou shalt hear me in the morning;
  Then will I thy throne address:
But in sin thou hast no pleasure;
  Thou wilt not the wicked bless.

Pride intensely thou abhorrest,
  Canst not blood and falsehood bear;
But through mercy, in thy presence
  Suffer me to offer prayer.

'Mid my foes, O Lord, direct me,
  From their cruel falsehoods save;
For their heart is full of malice,
  And their throat an open grave.

They their tongues employ to flatter,
  While my ruin they design;
Lord, confound thou their devices;
  They are enemies of thine:

But make joyful all who trust thee,
  Let them sing thy worthy praise;
For thou dost protect the righteous—
  Shield them all their earthly days.

PSALM VI.

Prayer in Distress.

SCOURGE me not, O Lord, in anger;
  By my weakness be impressed;
Heal me, for my bones all tremble,
  And my soul is sore distressed.

Now, O Lord, why dost thou tarry?
  Come, deliv'rance grant to me;
For in death no praise is offered—
  In the grave none worship thee.

I am weary with my groaning,
  Tears have made my couch to swim,
Till with grief by foes inflicted,
  Wasted is mine eye, and dim.

Leave me now, ye evil-doers,
  For I have acceptance found;
God my earnest prayer doth answer,
  And my foes repel, confound.

PSALM VII.

Prayer for Protection from Enemies.

O LORD, from my foes thou art mighty to save;
  In mercy my prayer be pleased now to hear,
Lest the enemy should like a fierce lion rave,
  And tear me in pieces while no help is near.

If I have with evil rewarded my friend,
  Or needlessly injured my merciless foe,
Let crushing affliction upon me descend,
  And instantly prone in the dust lay me low.

Arise now, O Lord, and my foes all confound;
  Thy power to avenge to the nations make known;
Let them in the judgment encompass thee round;
  For the sake of the righteous ascend thou thy throne!

But in equity judge me as I have been just;
  The schemes of the wicked at once overthrow,

And establish the righteous, for in thee they
    trust,
  Who triest all hearts, and all secrets dost
    know.

The Lord is the shield of the upright in heart;
  The wicked his anger provoke every day;
And from him at last he will bid them depart;
  His weapons of death shall them instantly
    slay.

The fruit of transgression disappointment shall
    be,
  And the pit him engulf by whom it is made;
But I, righteous Lord, praise shall offer to thee,
  In the work of thy praise thou wilt give me
    thine aid.

PSALM VIII.
God cares for Man.

O LORD, our Lord, in all the earth,
  How excellent thy name!
'Thou causest babes to speak thy praise,
  To put thy foes to shame.

Behold the heavens with stars begemmed,
  The work thy fingers wrought;
Contrasted with this gorgeous scene,
  Man may appear as nought.

But he was, in his first estate,
    Made little less than God;
Inferior creatures him obeyed,
    And trembled at his nod.

Thus thou didst him with honor crown,
    When from thy hand he came;
O Lord, our Lord, in all the earth,
    How excellent thy name!

PSALM IX.

Confidence in God's Mercy.

WITH my whole heart, O Lord, to thee
    In praise will I lift up my voice,
Thy works bid all the people see,
    And in thy faithfulness rejoice.

Mine enemies before thee fall,
    Who ever doth the just defend;
But nations who for vengeance call,
    Thou bringest to a shameful end!

Thus God reigns here in righteousness,
    And stands our shield and hiding-place;
Them he relieves whom foes oppress,
    And none forsakes who seek his face.

Then him address with thankful songs,
    And all his wondrous works declare;
For he avenges all our wrongs,
    And kindly hears our fervent prayer.

Not vainly, Lord, I cried to thee,—
    "Look on me in affliction's hour,
That I the gates of death may flee,
    To speak thy praise and saving power!"

The wicked, by their works ensnared,
    Give proof that thou dost reign supreme;
They for perdition are prepared—
    But thou the righteous wilt redeem.

Now rise, O Lord! the proud cast down,
    And forth to righteous judgment go;
Let the ungodly see thy frown!
    Themselves but men the nations know!

PSALM X.

The Authority of the Wicked Deprecated.

O LORD, why dost thou distant stand,
When times of trouble scourge the land?
Why from the poor and wretched hide,
When they writhe in the toils of pride?
Th' oppressor has his heart's desire,
All power to which he dare aspire;

He ever prospers in his way,
Escapes thy judgments day by day,
So that he says, "I shall not see
In all my days adversity."
He proudly of oppression speaks;
To slay the just in secret seeks;
As a fierce lion lies in wait
To bring the helpless to his fate;
And proudly says, "God hides his face,
Nor sees me from his holy place."

Arise, O Lord! lift up thy hand;
Protect the helpless in the land;
For though th' oppressor thinks it not,
Thou dost regard their cruel lot;
And on thy hand thou writest down
The features of his scornful frown!
And hence the poor and fatherless,
Turn ever to thee in distress.
Hurl, then, the wicked down from power,
And on him bring the vengeful hour!

The Lord, our King, on earth doth reign;
The wicked shall at last be slain;
For thou will lend a list'ning ear,
The voice of our distress to hear;
Us to protect stretch forth thy hand,
And guard us safely in the land.

PSALM XI.

The Righteous Protected and Wicked Punished.

ON God I my trust firmly stay;
   Then why cry ye out to my soul,—
"To the hills as a bird fly away,
   For the wicked reject thy control;
Even now they have bent the strong bow,
   On the string fixed the arrow aright,
That thee they may instantly slay,
   While securely concealed from thy sight."

If God suffer the powers he ordained
   On the earth to be all broken up—
If his people are thus to be slain,
   O what have the righteous to hope?
God dwells in his temple below,
   Though his throne is the measureless height!
And the righteous he tries for their good,
   But the wicked are vile in his sight.

And on them, in the day of his wrath,
   He will rain fire, and brimstone, and snares,
With tempest—death strewing its path—
   This for them is the cup he prepares.

But his nature, unchangeably just,
  Toward the righteous is holiest love;
And on them he complacently smiles—
  Makes their sky calm and cloudless above.

PSALM XII.
God faithful to his Word.

HELP, Lord, for the good man dies;
  He among the wicked fails;
While they utter artful lies,
  And his name their tongue assails.
They their flatt'ring lips employ
  To conceal a double heart;
Soon, O God, those lips destroy,
  For supremely just thou art.

In their vanity they say,
  "With our tongues we shall prevail;
Who is He we should obey?
  Our reliance cannot fail."
Then thou answerest, "I will
  For the sighing one stand up,
And his just desires fulfill;
  I will be his shield and hope."

All the words of God are pure,
  Like the silver most refined;
Hence they evermore are sure,
  Setting forth th' Eternal Mind.

Watching o'er them night and day,
    Thou wilt make them firmly stand;
Though abroad the wicked stray,
    And the vile control the land.

PSALM XIII.

Prayer and Trust.

HOW long, O Lord, wilt thou forget,
    And hide thy face from me?
How long shall care perplex my soul,
    Nor sorrow from me flee?

How long shall foes o'er me exult?
    O Lord, hear thou my voice,
Lest I should sleep the sleep of death,
    And them my fall rejoice.

Yet in thy goodness will I trust
    Through all my earthly days;
In thy salvation make my boast,
    And sing thy worthy praise.

PSALM XIV.

Universal Depravity.

SAYS the heart of the foolish ones, "There is no God!"
    They all are corrupt and have hateful things done;

Though great is their number, not one doeth
   good;
   God looked down from heaven, and he could
   find none.

None fully their duty to God understand,
   But all with delight into wickedness run;
Corrupt is our race throughout all the land,
   There is none that good doeth; no, not even
   one.

But shall not all they who in sin take delight,
   Who, hating God's people, fiercely devour,
And shunning his worship, bow not in his
   sight,
   Be judged in the end, and feel his dread
   power?

Ah! then shall they tremble before him in fear;
   But the righteous he will more abundantly
   bless;
For though they now meet with derision and
   sneer,
   Their refuge he stands in the day of distress.

O that out of Zion salvation would come
   To them thou didst ransom, the race of thy
   choice!

When thine exiles on earth thou at last shalt
    bring home,
They then shall praise thee, and in gladness
    rejoice.

PSALM XV.

Who will be Saved?

WHO in thy tabernacle, Lord,
    Shall ever dwell secure?
Who stand on Zion's holy hill,
    And ev'ry test endure?

He that is righteous in his way,
    And truth explicit speaks;
That not by word nor deed of his,
    Another's injury seeks;

He that approves not persons vile,
    As them that fear the Lord;
That having promised, changes not,
    But sacred holds his word;

He that lends not at usury,
    Nor takes a bribe for gain;
He, saved by grace divine, with thee
    Shall evermore remain.

PSALM XVI.

Rejoicing in God's Goodness.

PRESERVE me, O God, for in thee do I trust;
  Yea, thou art my Lord, and the source of my joys;
While the good in the land, the holy and just,
  Afford me delight no deception alloys.

But they who bow down at an idol's false shrine
  Shall have sorrows increased—all that stern justice claims!
Their drink-offerings of blood I will never make mine,
  Nor even my lips pollute with their names.

The Lord is my portion unchangeably good;
  Secure is my right by the kind will of Heaven;
The lines to me fallen pleasant places include;
  A goodly inheritance me has been given.

I will my Protector now fervently praise,
  Having been in night-seasons instructed, reproved;
I will to thy worship devote all my days;
  With thee by my side I shall never be moved.

Hence glad is my heart, firmly resting in hope;
  I am guarded by thee, who art mighty to save;
To death thou wilt never my spirit give up,
  Nor thy Holy One suffer to waste in the grave.

And I shall, 'mid the wand'rings my brief days employ,
  In the sure path of life by thy guidance be found;
Then rise where thy presence gives fullness of joy,
  For at thy right hand living pleasures abound.

PSALM XVII.

Confident Supplication.

HEAR, O Lord, the cause of justice;
  Listen to my prayer sincere;
From thee let me hear my sentence—
  May thy lips pronounce me clear:
    And uprightness
  To thine eye in me appear.

Me in night's calm stillness visit;
  Try me as the gold is tried;

Thou shalt find no wrong intention,
   For thy word has been my guide:
     But support me,
That secure I may abide.

Now I call, for thou will hear me;
   Now to thee for refuge fly:
In the hour of danger guard me
   As the apple of thine eye!
     'Neath the shadow
Of thy wings secure I lie.

Me my deadly foes encompass;
   Fierce, malignant, vile are they;
All my steps intently watching,
   That they me may lead astray:
     As a lion,
Seek they eagerly their prey.

Rise, O Lord, and me deliver
   From the wicked by thy sword!
They in this life have their portion;
   They on earth their treasures hoard,
     And their children
Leave the wealth their toil has stored.

But through righteousness imputed,
   I shall rise thy smiles to share;

Rich for ever in thy favor,
  Naught beside shall wish or care,
    Satisfied when
  I thy glorious image bear.

PSALM XVIII.

The Lord of Sabaoth in Action.

O LORD, my strength, my rock, my tower,
Thee do I trust in danger's hour;
And on thee place my ardent love,
For still thy constancy I prove.
Thou worthy art of our best praise,
For thou dost guard us all our days.
Dangers on every side I found,
The snares of death me compassed round,
Upon me poured the floods of wrath,
The snares of hell beset my path;
But to my God for help I prayed,
And earnest supplication made;
And from his royal throne on high,
His ears attended to my cry.

His wrath then caused the earth to quake;
The mountain's firm foundations shake,
For, coming to destroy my foes,
Smoke densely from his nostrils rose;

His mouth poured forth the fires of wrath,
The lightnings shot along his path;
The heavens he bowed, 'mid clouds appeared,
While vapor 'neath his feet careered.
He swiftly on a cherub rode,
The wind its wings on him bestowed,
And darkness gathered round his head,
As he his dense pavillion spread.

But the bright beaming of his face,
The clouds to distant regions chase;
Then coals of fire—intensest flame,
With hail-stones, from his presence came!
His voice was heard along the sky,
His arrows did unerring fly.
My foes were scattered far and near,
Slaughtered, or overcome by fear!
At thy rebuke, O Lord, the blast—
The breath that from thy nostrils passed,
The sea its channels deep displayed,
And earth's foundations bare were laid!
His hand he reached down from above,
And me, the object of his love,
Drew from the deep where I lay low,
And saved me from the cruel foe.
They triumphed in an evil day;
But still the Lord was my firm stay;

And he was pleased my prayer to hear,
And graciously enlarge my sphere.

Thus God has me been pleased to bless
According to my righteousness;
For all his laws were in my sight,
To keep them was my chief delight;
And he deals with his creatures here
As in his sight their ways appear:
Is merciful, upright, and pure,
With them whose lives such acts insure;
But soon or later sends his curse
On such as are of ways perverse;
The people saves who in him trust,
But lays the haughty in the dust.
He has my darkness chased away,
My lamp made brilliant as the day,
Me given strength through troops to break,
And leap over walls the prize to take.

The ways of God are just and true,
His work has purging fire passed through;
He is their shield who in him trust—
The Lord for ever good and just;
Our rock in danger's direst hour,
Who kindly girded me with power,

Made plain my path, my feet to climb
To a position high, sublime;
And taught my hands in war to fight,
To bend the bow of brass aright.
While o'er my head he was my shield,
His hand sustained me in the field;
His goodness stooped to make me great,
And guard me from an evil fate;
So that I safely chased the foe,
And in the dust soon laid them low.
He smote their hearts as I drew near,
At once with strange, subduing fear:
And me endowed with strength to meet,
And trample them beneath my feet.
In vain for help to God they cried;
Protection he to them denied,
Till I could them no longer find—
Made like the dust before the wind!

Thus nations at my feet were laid,
For o'er them God had made me head;
In his wise rule ordained that they
Who knew me not should me obey;
While strangers wasted far and near,
And in their strongholds quaked with fear.
God ever lives, my rock most blessed!
Be fervent praise to him addressed!

He nations has to me subdued,
And saved me from the man of blood!
My adversaries overcome,
And smote my foes with terror dumb.
Hence thanks, O Lord, thy favors claim—
Ye nations praise his holy name.
He reigns supreme, forever lives,
And to me kind deliverance gives—
Has greater gifts for me in store—
Will bless and save me evermore.

PSALM XIX.

God's Glory in his Works and Word.

THE glory of God the heavens display,
    The firmament his works of light;
Day gives instruction unto day,
    And night shows knowledge unto night:
Though they have not the power of speech,
Their voice earth's utmost limits reach.

A tent he spreads there for the sun,
    Which comes forth as a bridegroom gay;
Rejoices his grand course to run,
    Strong to complete it in a day!
And while he his vast circuit shapes,
Naught from his searching heat escapes.

God's perfect law revives the soul,
　His precepts make the simple wise,
His statutes bless whom they control,
　And his commands delight our eyes:
The service of the Lord is pure,
And shall for evermore endure.

God's judgments righteous are and true,
　More precious than the finest gold;
While to the saints, his will who do,
　Their sweetness never can be told!
They ever place us on our guard,
And keeping them gives great reward.

But who can his offenses know?
　From secret faults, O cleanse thou me!
Restrain when I astray would go,
　From sins presumptuous keep me free:
Then shall my life be pure and right,
And unpolluted in thy sight.

To me, O Lord, thy grace impart,
　That all my words, truthful and kind,
And meditations of my heart,
　May in thy sight acceptance find!
For help before thy throne I bow—
My strength and my Redeemer, thou.

PSALM XX.

Intercession for a Ruler.

THE Lord hear thee in the evil day,
The God of Jacob be thy stay;
Help from his sanctuary send,
And strength from Zion thee attend.
May God thy offerings regard,
Thy sacrifices all reward,
And grant thee all thy heart's desire,
Which right and holiness inspire.
We in thy safety will rejoice,
To God in praise lift up our voice,
And in his name will triumph still,
If he again thy prayers fulfill.

God helps his servant, now I know;
From heaven regards him here below;
With saving strength of his right hand,
Him causes still secure to stand.
Some in their martial forces boast;
But we trust in the Lord of hosts.
They fell before the griding sword;
But we stood, guarded by the Lord.
Hear us again, on thee we call,
And let no evil us befall.

PSALM XXI.

Praise for Victory.

THE king rejoices in thy strength, O Lord,
And the protection thou dost him afford.
With all his heart's desire thou hast him blessed,
Nor him denied one suitable request.
Thou richest blessings hast around him spread,
And with a golden crown bedecked his head.
Of thee he asked for life; thou didst it give—
Yea, promised that he evermore should live.
Great is his glory through thy sacred aid;
Honor and majesty are on him laid;
And nothing shall his happy state destroy;
But thy kind smiles o'erflow his heart with joy.
The Lord, to whose fidelity he trusted all,
Will kindly order that he ne'er shall fall.

Thy mighty hand thy foes shall overtake:
Thy wrath them as a burning oven make!
God shall them swallow in his kindled ire,
And them devote to the devouring fire!
Even their offspring thou shall give no place,
But from the earth destroy the wicked race.
They spread their nets thee slyly to assail;
They plotted mischief, but did not prevail:

And they shall from thee fly, senseless to shame,
When thou dost deadly arrows at them aim!
O Lord, thyself exalt by thy great might!
So shall we ever in thy praise delight.

PSALM XXII.

PART I.

Description of Christ's Crucifixion.

MY God, my God, O why forsake thou me?
　This is a sad and darkly evil day!
In deep distress I vainly cry to thee,
　And even in the night unheard I pray.

Yet thou art good—the high and holy One,
　'Mid Israel's praises dwelling evermore!
Of those who trust thee disappointing none,
　And having for them blessings rich in store.

But in the flesh I as a worm am made;
　At me the people rudely scoff and rave:
"He trusted God, let him afford him aid,
　And from this hour of fearful darkness save."

O God, thou didst my earthly being give;
　I in my mother's arms to thee was dear;
And still I through thy tender mercy live—
　Why stand aloof when torture now is near?

As maddened wild beasts me the wicked throng;
　To utter lies their mouths they open wide;
From them I have so much received of wrong,
　My strength is as an earthen vessel dried!

They without pity pierce my hands and feet,
　And standing round, me searching glances give;
Divide my garments as to them seems meet,
　And cast lots which my vesture shall receive.

Be near, O Thou, who gavest me my breath;
　Thou art my hope and strength; make haste to save;
My life deliver from the mouth of death,
　My body snatch from the devouring grave!

PART II.

Descriptive of Christ's Kingdom.

I WILL, O Lord, adore thy holy name,
　And in the congregation sing thy praise;
Ye saints, extol him, yea, his grace proclaim,
　And fear before him all your earthly days.

For he despises not the low and plaintive cry,
　Nor from the poor and suffering hides his face;

The humble may to him in prayer draw nigh,
   And all who come may find his helping grace.

And at his table shall th' afflicted eat,
   Till satisfied with bounties rich and free;
And they who seek God, round his altar meet,
   And in his worship ever joyful be.

To him all people shall devoutly turn,
   The families all worship him again:
For they, ere long, Messiah's name shall learn,
   And he o'er all the happy nations reign.

Earth's rich and mighty, with supreme delight,
   Shall eat and worship in his house below;
The dying on him fix their eager sight,
   And, trusting, to his glorious presence go.

And thus each generation in its day,
   To the succeeding shall his name declare;
Until the saints the world shall firmly sway,
   And all the people countless mercies share.

PSALM XXIII.

Christ the Good Shepherd.

ME Jesus, the good Shepherd, feeds;
   I shall not be by want oppressed;
Beside still waters me he leads,
   And in green pastures gives me rest.

And if my spirit's strength decay,
   He leaves me not my loss to moan;
But guides me in the righteous way,
   For sake of merit all his own.

Yea, and no evil need I fear,
   Though I pass through death's gloomy vale;
For Jesus there will still be near—
   His kind support can never fail.

He richly doth my table spread,
   To shame the counsel of my foes;
The oil of gladness crowns my head,
   With holy joy my cup o'erflows.

And surely thus his goodness will
   Attend me all my earthly days;
Then bring me safe to Zion's hill,
   Where I shall ever sing his praise.

PSALM XXIV.

Ascension of Christ.

THE earth, with all its store of wealth,
   O Lord, belongs to thee,
Whose sov'reign, universal will
   Controls the land and sea:
But who shall thy high throne ascend,
   And take the kingdom ne'er to end?

He of clean hands, and pure of heart,
    Who hath no evil done;
Nor falsehood told, nor falsely sworn,
    Our Saviour, God the Son:
'Tis he ascends now to his throne,
And claims the kingdom as his own.

Lift up your heads, ye lofty gates!
    Ye massive doors, unfold!
Let ye the glorious King come in,
    And take the crown of gold!
Who is the King of glory? He
Who died to set the captives free.

Then lift your heads, ye lofty gates!
    Ye massive doors, fly wide!
Let ye the glorious King come in,
    For he for sinners died!
Who is the King of glory? He
Who won from death the victory!

PSALM XXV.

Prayer for Divine Guidance.

I LIFT my soul, O Lord, to thee;
Forbid that shame my lot should be,
    Or that my foes should me o'ertake;

Let only those be put to shame
Who, hoping not in thy great name,
   Thy worship wickedly forsake!

Teach me the way that I should go,
Let me thy truth and goodness know,
   For all my help must come from thee:
Be thou to mercy still inclined,
Call not my youthful faults to mind,
   But kindly still remember me.

Thou merciful and gracious art
To those who from thy ways depart,
   And wouldst them back to thee receive;
And thou art just, and wilt repay
Those who ne'er from thy precepts stray,
   And them thy bounties richly give.

Who fears thee, Lord, and in thy ways
Delights; through all his earthly days,
   He and his offspring shall be blessed!
Hence would I claim thee for my friend—
To me thy kind deliverance send,
   And let me in thy goodness rest.

O bid my sorrows all depart,
Lighten the burdens of my heart,
   And grant me now thy pard'ning grace;

Then me defend, sustain me still,
That I may ever do thy will,
   Securely kept by thine embrace.

PSALM XXVI.

Desire to be with God's People.

JUDGE me, O Lord, for thou art just;
And hence in thee I put my trust—
   Mine inmost nature prove!
Thy kindness is before mine eyes;
I do not take delight in lies,
   Nor any evil love.

I wash my hands from every stain,
And to thine altar come again,
   And lift my voice in praise:
I love thy temple, O my God,
The honored place of thine abode!
   And there would spend my days.

Gather me not with sinners, then;
To pass my days with cruel men,
   In blood who take delight;
Whose hands are full of bribes, to win
The innocent to ways of sin,
   Would my whole being blight!

Hence, gracious Saviour, help thou me
To walk in mine integrity,
  And me from sin redeem,
Then as I pass amid the land,
Or in the congregation stand,
  Thy praise shall be my theme.

PSALM XXVII.
Rejoicing in Christ.

WHEN my Saviour is near
I have nothing to fear
For then he is my shield and my tower;
  He has vanquished the foes
  Which against me arose,
And I'll trust him till life's latest hour.

Now to this I aspire
As my highest desire,
To abide in his house all my days;
  And there ever behold
  All its glories untold,
And on thee, my Redeemer, to gaze.

And me then he will hide,
Clasping close to his side,
Till the storms are all over and passed;
  While my voice I will raise
  In the songs of his praise,
And that learn which forever shall last.

Thou wilt hear when I pray,
Thou wilt call when I stray,
And again me to favor receive;
But, O hide not thy face,
And withhold not thy grace,
Nor me once to my helplessness leave!

Thou, O Lord, art my hope,
And me thou wilt take up,
Should my friends on the earth me forsake;
And though foes should arise,
And my ruin devise,
Thou will teach me the path I should take.

Thou art righteous and just;
And thy goodness I trust
In the land of the living to see;
But make thou my heart strong,
And more joyful my song,
While still hoping, I wait upon thee.

PSALM XXVIII.

Cast me not off with the Wicked.

TO thee, O Lord, I cry;
Do not my suit deny,
Lest I should see no more the light of day;

I to thy temple flee,
And lift my hands to thee—
O with the wicked cast me not away!

They seem as seems a friend,
While mischief they intend;
But thou at last them their desert wilt give;
For they against thee fight,
Nor in thy works delight—
And shall they here in happy quiet live?

O, thou hast heard my prayer;
I shall thy mercies share—
Thou wilt protect and guide me all my days;
Thy people, too, shall stand,
And prosper in the land;
Hence joyfully I sing thy worthy praise.

PSALM XXIX.
God's Glory seen in a Thunder-storm.

SONS of God, arise and give
Praise to Him by whom ye live!
Give the Lord praise due his name!
In his temple speak his fame!

The voice of God along the shore
Louder sounds than ocean's roar!
Thunders now the Lord above—
Sounds that o'er the waters move.

O the voice of God is strong!
Rolls in majesty along!
It the lofty cedar breaks;
It the mighty mountain shakes!

Lo! the mountains seem to bound;
Leap they, startled by the sound!
Dance they wildly, as in play,
Ravished by some joyful lay!

Now the utt'rance of his ire
Cuts from clouds the flames of fire;
Flash the lightnings wildly forth,
Dart along the trembling earth.

Hinds the wild confusion hear,
And are overcome with fear;
Tempests lay the forests bare,
Trees and boughs unseemly tear!

All these things on high, below,
God's amazing glory show;
While he sits the storm above,
Still th' unchanging God of love!

Yea, he reigns for evermore,
On the earth from shore to shore;
He will strength in us increase,
He will bless his saints with peace.

PSALM XXX.

An Offering of Praise.

I WILL extol my Saviour,
   For he has raised me up,
When near the grave he found me;
   And granted me my hope.

His anger lasts a moment,
   His smiles through life remain;
Grief all the night may tarry,
   But morn brings joy again.

O'er me my foes' rejoicing
   He turned to bitter shame!
Hence songs I bring before him,
   And praise his holy name.

I once said, when elated,
   "I shall securely rest;"
But he his face hid from me,
   And left me sore distressed:

Then I made supplication:
   "Can dust thy truth declare?
Or can my death thee profit?"
   And he received my prayer.

He turned my grief to gladness;
    To comeliness my shame:
Hence songs I bring before him,
    And praise his holy name.

PSALM XXXI.

PART I.

Prayer in Distress.

O LORD, I in thy goodness trust;
    Now hear me while I pray;
Be thou my rock when danger's near,
    My guide when dark my way.

Be thou my strength to set me free
    When foes my feet ensnare:
To shun their lying vanities
    Let truth my soul prepare.

Then will I, through thy grace, rejoice
    That thou hast look'd on me;
Nor to my foes me given up,
    But from them set me free.

But now I am consumed of grief,
    My neighbors' scorn and dread!
They shun me when abroad I move—
    Forget me as one dead!

With fears I am encompassed round,
    While sland'rous words they say,
And enter into counsel vile
    To take my life away.

But thee I trust; thou art my God;
    My life is in thy hand;
Deliver me from my distress—
    Protect me in the land.

PART II.

Comfort of God's People.

LET but the vile be put to shame,
    Their sudden death allowed;
Be but the lips to silence put
    Which speak false words and proud.

Great goodness hast thou treasured up,
    And dost thy people show;
Thou hidest them with thee secure
    From every artful foe.

Praised be the Lord, he has me blessed;
    As a fenced city made;
Relieved me when I was distressed,
    Encouraged when afraid.

Then love the Lord, ye humble ones,
   For he the proud repays;
Be of good courage, strong your hearts,
   And trust him all your days.

PSALM XXXII.

The Penitent Pardoned.

HAPPY the pardoned soul
   In Heaven's complacent smile!
It is set free from sin's control,
   And dispossessed of guile.

I greatly was distressed,
   Nor slightest peace could see,
Till I at last my sin confessed—
   My great iniquity.

God saw my sin-sick soul
   By grief brought near the grave;
His gentle voice pronounced me whole,
   And all my sins forgave.

The floods shall not o'erflow
   The soul to God that prays;
He hides me from the cruel foe,
   And fills my mouth with praise.

He kind instruction gives,
   And keeps on me his eye;
Into his presence he receives,
   And to him brings me nigh.

The wicked are distressed;
   The saints have sweet employ:
For they of God are greatly blessed—
They shout aloud for joy.

PSALM XXXIII.

God our Creator, Governor, and Protector.

IN the Lord, ye saints, rejoice;
Lift to him your tuneful voice,
And the harp enchanting bring;
To the great Jehovah sing.
Let all bow his throne before,
And his name again adore;
It becomes us all our days
Joyfully to sing his praise.

All the words of God are right,
All his acts proclaim his might;
Righteousness in man he wills,
And the earth with goodness fills.

He the heavens above us made,
All the glory there displayed,
And the waters of the deep
Gathered like a garnered heap.

Come, ye nations, every land,
And with awe before him stand.
He is the Almighty One,
For he spake, and it was done;
He commanded, it stood fast!
He can all the nations blast.
Ever shall his reign endure,
And his purposes are sure.

But the righteous are alone
Chosen by him for his own;
And on them with purest love,
Looks he ever from above.
Lo! the nations to his gaze
Are exposed through all their days;
And he only by his power,
Saves in peril's dreadful hour.

When opposing hosts engage,
And contending forces rage,

The hero by his mercy lives—
God alone protection gives.
He looks kindly on the just;
All who in his goodness trust,
He forbids death should them kill,
And in famine feeds them still.

Hence he is our constant hope,
And our souls to him look up;
He is our abiding shield,
We are by his mercy sealed;
And in him our hearts rejoice,
While in praise we lift our voice.
Let thy goodness, Lord most just,
Be on us as thee we trust!

PSALM XXXIV.

PART I.

God Blesses and Protects his People.

I WILL the great Jehovah bless,
　And ever speak his praise;
Boast in his truth and righteousness
　Through all my earthly days.

Hear, ye afflicted, and rejoice,
　And magnify his name;

Let us together raise our voice,
   And his great love proclaim.

I sought the Lord in fervent prayer,
   He listened to my cry;
To save me from my fear and care,
   Through grace I found him nigh.

Look then to him in your distress;
   God will give light divine;
The rising Sun of Righteousness
   Your faces cause to shine.

The angels of the Lord descend,
   And all the saints inclose;
They them in danger's hour defend,
   And save them from their foes.

O taste and see that God is good!
   He will his favors grant;
The beasts of prey may lack for food,
   But ye no good shall want.

PART II.

The Penitent Encouraged.

COME ye who will instruction hear,
   The words of truth receive;
They will you teach the Lord to fear,
   And in his ways to live.

He who desires life's full reward,
　And Heaven's continued smile,
Let him his tongue from evil guard,
　His lips from speaking guile.

God on the just looks kindly down,
　And hears their pious claims;
But on the wicked turns his frown—
　Blots from the earth their names!

The penitent and broken heart
　He is divinely near;
Vouchsafes sweet comfort to impart,
　And dry the falling tear.

And though, oft-times, afflictions great
　The righteous may befall,
Yet God for ever guards their fate—
　Delivers from them all.

But they who causeless hate the just,
　Shall God's dread judgments slay!
While his rich mercies crown the trust
　Of those who him obey.

PSALM XXXV.

PART I.

Prayer concerning Secret Foes.

O LORD, take hold of shield and buckler,
　Contend against my cruel foes;

The spear and ax wield thou against them,
    My persecutors all oppose.

Soon let them be disgraced, confounded;
    Drive them like dust before the wind—
Chased by the angel of Jehovah,
    Against whom greatly they have sinned!

They without cause have snares laid for me,
    Sought secretly me to enthrall;
Let unforeseen destruction seize them!
    In their own ruin let them fall!

Then will I boast in thy protection;
    "Who's like the Lord?" my soul shall say:
"The weak he rescues from th' oppressor,
    The spoiler makes his easy prey!"

PART II.

Prayer concerning False Witnesses.

FALSE witnesses rose up against me,
    Asserting what ne'er crossed my mind;
For good they have returned me evil,
    For help, my overthrow designed.

Yet for their sickness I wore sackcloth,
    And offered for them fervent prayer;
As one when mourning for his mother,
    I grief endured above my share.

Still doth my fall give them rejoicing,
  Extreme delight distress instead;
At me their teeth intently gnashing,
  As men who basely mock for bread!

How long, O Lord, wilt thou behold this?
  O for my rescue now appear!
Then will I in the great assembly
  Thee offer praise with heart sincere.

PART III.

Prayer concerning Public Crimes.

FORBID my foes should triumph o'er me:
  They seek not quiet in the land:
O Lord, thou seest: be not silent—
  Thou dost their mocking understand.

From them thy servant soon deliver;
  Judge me in truth and righteousness;
Let them not say, "We have our longing—
  We have him brought to deep distress!"

Clothe them with shame and ignominy,
  But let my friends in thee rejoice;
So shall my lips pronounce thee righteous,
  And long thy praise employ my voice.

PSALM XXXVI.

PART I.

Description of the Wicked.

TO speak about his guilt extreme
   Who has in grace no saving part
Is a sad duty; yet this theme
   I find now pressing on my heart.

He has, him to restrain from crime,
   No fear of God before his eyes,
But wickedly misspends his time
   As his vile nature may devise.

Himself he flatters that his ways
   Are quite as good as there is need;
He shuns the light through all his days—
   The truth he hears he does not heed.

His words his purposes disguise,
   Nor his deceit and guilt declare;
He makes no effort to be wise,
   And to do good is not his care.

In night's lone hour, while others sleep,
   He crime and mischief meditates;
Himself from vice seeks not to keep,
   And sin not for a moment hates.

PART II.

God his People's Defense.

THY goodness, Lord, abroad expands;
  Thy faithfulness mounts to the sky;
Thy righteousness more firmly stands
  Than do the mountains, strong and high.

Thy judgments are a mighty deep;
  Thy care o'er all the earth extends;
Thou for thy saints dost blessings keep,
  Thy mercy ever them defends.

Beneath the shadow of thy wings,
  Safe they who there for refuge fly;
Th' abundance from thy house which springs,
  Shall all their longings satisfy.

They unrestrained drink from the stream
  Of joys which issues from thy throne;
Thy cheering light doth on them beam;
  The life divine is their's alone.

O let thy loving-kindness still
  Thy saints upon the earth attend;
Help them to do thy righteous will,
  And ever from their foes defend.

PSALM XXXVII.

PART I.

The Righteous Exhorted to Trust in God.

LET not the wicked thee provoke,
   Nor envy in thy heart excite;
For they shall fall by one dread stroke,
   And quickly wither in thy sight.

Then in the Lord put thou thy trust,
   And seek the ways of righteousness;
For kindly he regards the just,
   And will with his rich favors bless.

Yea, cast thy cares upon the Lord,
   Who never will thy trust betray,
But thee abundant grace afford—
   Thy justice to the world display.

Repose on God, and calmly wait,
   Though vice should for a time succeed;
Do not the wicked imitate,
   Nor hopeful do an evil deed.

For cursed shall they be in the land;
   Soon shall their place no more be found;
But for the just God will command
   That peace and plenty shall abound.

PART II.

God Defends the Righteous.

THE vile cannot the just abide,
　But madly gnash their teeth in hate;
Yet God doth all their plans deride,
　For he beholds their coming fate!

The wicked seek the just to slay,
　And hence their deadly weapons take;
But to them they shall fall a prey—
　Their weapons in their hands shall break.

Better the little of the just
　Than the abundance of the vile!
The wicked God will from him thrust,
　But on the righteous sweetly smile.

He for the upright kindly cares,
　And blesses all which they possess;
Against the evil day prepares,
　That famine may not them distress.

The righteous show a bounteous hand;
　The wicked borrowed goods withhold:
They shall be rooted from the land—
　Their ruin shall the just behold.

PART III.

God Prospers the Righteous.

THE good man's steps the Lord directs—
    Is pleased that he secure should stand;
All his missteps he soon corrects,
    And kindly holds him by the hand.

I have not once, where'er I've been,
    Though hoary age now crowns my head,
In friendless want the righteous seen,
    Nor yet his offspring begging bread.

Let all thy acts in life be right,
    Then thou shalt ever dwell secure;
For God in thee will take delight,
    And make to thee his mercies sure.

The wicked God will ne'er defend—
    Their offspring, even, shall not stand!
But he the righteous will attend,
    And give them to possess the land.

PART IV.

God Sustains and Saves the Righteous.

THE righteous man wise counsel gives,
    His lips words right and prudent say;
His heart the law of God receives,
    His footsteps firmly keep his way.

Against him though the wicked rise,
  He shall in perfect safety stand;
Yea, they shall fall before his eyes,
  And leave him to possess the land.

I've seen the wicked man in power,
  Like th' cedar reaching far around;
But while I gazed he was no more!
  I sought him, but he was not found.

Mark thou the righteous all his days,
  His end at last is perfect peace!
The wicked perish in their ways—
  Yea, soon in all the land they cease.

Salvation, coming from the Lord,
  He has appointed for the just;
And he will his kind help afford
  To all who in his mercy trust.

PSALM XXXVIII.

Prayer of Penitence.

LORD, rebuke me not in anger,
  Though my sins thy wrath demand;
Now thine arrows deeply pierce me;
  Heavy on me is thy hand.

In my flesh there is no soundness,
　　Sorely is my soul depressed;
For my sins in grief o'erwhelm me—
　　As a burden on me rest.

In mine own eyes I am loathsome,
　　To the earth am I bowed down;
All the day long do I go mourning;
　　I am tortured by thy frown!

But my longing, Lord, thou knowest;
　　My distress is seen by thee;
Lo! my heart now pants through weakness—
　　Light mine eyes refuse to see!

Former friends now all forsake me,
　　Foes lay snares along my way;
And they threaten my destruction—
　　Act deceitful all the day.

Yet do I refrain from speaking,
　　Seem as one that does not hear;
While on thee my soul reposes;
　　For thou wilt incline thine ear.

Let them never have occasion
　　Of rejoicing by my fall!
Now to thee I make confession—
　　Now for help on thee I call.

They are strong and greatly flourish;
  Lo, they rapidly increase!
Though they good repay with evil,
  Still I seek the way of peace.

O may I not be forsaken,
  Do not at a distance stand;
Visit me with thy salvation;
  Now to me extend thine hand.

PSALM XXXIX.

PART I.

The Vanity of Human Life.

BEFORE the wicked I resolved
  That I would guard my way,
And not my tongue employ in speech,
  Lest they my words gainsay.

For I had thought how time sweeps by
  Like a resistless flood;
And then was I with silence dumb—
  I spake not even good.

But silence caused intenser pain,
  Till all my peace had fled;
Then burst the fires of anguish forth,
  And earnestly I said:

"O Lord, make me to know mine end;
 My days how soon they pass;
Give me to see how frail I am—
 I wither as the grass.

"As a handbreadth is all my life;
 'Tis nothing in thy sight;
Man is at best but vanity—
 Day's soon-departing light!

"Disquiets he himself in vain,
 And riches treasures up;
But while he thus for nothing toils,
 O Lord, thou art my hope."

PART II.

A Prayer in Sickness.

WHEN in affliction's fearful hour,
 With wasting illness weak,
I saw how frail is human life,
 My tongue refused to speak.

O Lord, my grievous sins forgive,
 And lift on me thy smile;
And scoffers all to silence put,
 Who stand and me revile.

Thy dread infliction, too, remove,
　The stroke 'neath which I lay;
For when thou scourgest man for sin,
　His glory wastes away.

Ah! surely man is vanity—
　Me who can help but thee?
Do thou, to whom I offer prayer,
　My tears and anguish see.

As were my fathers, so am I,
　A brief sojourner here;
A stranger wand'ring to and fro,
　With warring hope and fear.

O spare me, thou by whom I live,
　And strength to me restore;
For hence ere long must I depart,
　And be on earth no more.

PSALM XL.

PART I.

The Sinner Saved.

IN a dismal pit I lay
Sinking in the miry clay;
But on God I waited there,
Patiently, in silent prayer.

He attentive, from on high,
Listened to my plaintive cry;
And in condescending love,
Gently caught me from above.

From the pit he brought me up,
Filled my heart with joyful hope;
Raised me by his drawings sweet,
On a rock made sure my feet.

Him to serve he made me strong;
Gave to me a joyful song,
Even a new song of praise,
Which I'll sing through all my days.

Many my escape shall see,
And, my Saviour, trust in thee;
While they to thy throne draw near,
And thee serve with filial fear.

Happy he who trusts in God—
In the Saviour's precious blood,
Rather than in men, for aid,
Who have false pretensions made.

PART II.

The Work of Redemption.

MANY works thou, Lord, hast done;
Wonderful are every one!

All thy purposes are kind—
They cannot be called to mind.

None to thee can be compared;
None thy glory yet has shared;
But demands the highest place
'Mid thy works, the work of grace!

God could never take delight
In the sacrificial rite;
And though hecatombs were slain,
They could not his favor gain.

But the Saviour said, "Behold,
Now I come, as long foretold;
Sinners I to God will draw,
Magnify and keep the law.

By the right will I abide,
I will not his justice hide,
But his faithfulness make known—
Mercy leads me to atone!

And my heralds shall proclaim
Through the world a Saviour's name;
My rich grace they shall possess,
Teach the way of righteousness.

PART III.

Prayer in Temptation.

LORD, do not from me withhold
Mercy which has been of old!
Evils have me compassed round,
Me my sin at last has found.

O my sins are numberless!
Me involving in distress;
But, O Lord, thy mercy give;
Let me in thy favor live.

May my constant, subtile foe,
Who would me involve in woe,
And my very life devour,
Be defeated by thy power!

Be the tempter driven back,
As he comes me to attack;
But may all the saints rejoice—
In thy praise employ their voice.

Though I am a suff'rer here,
To my cry God turns his ear;
Come, my Saviour, now, I pray;
Me to bless make no delay.

PSALM XLI.

PART I.

The Reward of Charity.

HE who the suff'ring poor
    Of his abundance gives,
Nor rudely spurns them from his door,
    Reward on earth receives.

If troubles round him press,
    Him God will then set free;
And in the hour of sad distress
    His comforter will be.

If dangers throng his way,
    From them God will protect;
Deliver from the evil day—
    In mercy him correct.

If foes should him assail,
    And seek to take his life,
They shall not over him prevail,
    But end in shame their strife.

If sickness waste his frame,
    God then will give him rest;
In all things we may think or name,
    He shall be greatly blessed.

PART II.

Deceitful Foes and Treacherous Friends.

BE merciful, O God,
    And hear my earnest prayer;
O'er me spread thy protection broad,
    And from the wicked spare.

Though friendship they pretend,
    And me their visits make,
In them deceit and malice blend;
    Abroad they falsehoods speak.

They hatred clearly show,
    And my defeat devise;
They whisper, "He has fallen low,
    And shall no more arise."

Yea, and through their deceit,
    My friend, who by my side
Oft did at mine own table eat,
    Has with my foes allied.

O God, my cause defend;
    Defeat my cruel foes;
Be thou my sure, abiding friend,
    And give me sweet repose.

BOOK II.

PSALMS XLII and XLIII.

Longing after God.

AS pants the hart for water brooks,
  So pants my soul, O God, for thee:
Yea, for the living God I thirst;
  O when shall I his glory see?
My tears have been my daily food,
While scoffers ask, Where is thy God?
And glancing o'er the past again,
My soul flows out in wasting pain;
For I had gone with joyful lay
With those who fain keep holy day.
But why, my soul, art thou cast down?
Why bowed beneath the foe's dread frown?
Hope thou in God, and sing his praise;
His presence will prolong my days.

Yet sorely is my soul depressed;
  In exile from thy house of prayer,
Thee will I make my constant rest,
  And call to mind thy mercies there.

Deep calls to deep, for storm now raves,
And o'er me drives impetuous waves!
Still God will be my song by night,
By day. my trust and chief delight,
Though now I feel th' oppressor's rod,
And scoffers ask, " Where is thy God ? "
But why, my soul, art thou cast down ?
Why bowed beneath the foe's dread frown ?
Hope thou in God, and sing his praise;
His presence will prolong my days.

Judge me, O God, and plead my cause;
   O save me from the cruel foe!
Thou art my strength—why cast me off?
   Why should I still thus mourning go?
O send thy light abroad as flame,
To all around thy truth proclaim,
That they may gently lead me still,
And bring me to thy holy hill;
Where praise shall my best hours employ
Before thee, my exceeding joy!
Why then, my soul, art thou cast down?
Why bowed beneath the foe's dread frown?
Hope thou in God, and sing his praise;
His presence will prolong my days.

PSALM XLIV.

PART I.

Praise for National Independence.

O LORD, our ears have heard
Words which our hearts have stirred;
Our fathers have us told
Thy works in days of old;
How thou didst them with kindness bless,
And crown their arms with great success!

Thou didst with thine own hand
Drive our foes from the land,
And plant our fathers here,
Safe from distressing fear;
And give them great prosperity,
And make them 'mid the nations free!

Not by their might did they
In battle gain the day,
And this fair land possess,
With no foe to oppress;
But thou didst thine own arm extend,
And them against their foes defend!

Thou art, O God, our King!
And we thy mercies sing;
For in each time of need
We shall through Thee succeed;

And ever triumph o'er our foes—
Safe while we in thy power repose!

And Thou art now our shield,
To guard us in the field,
While a disastrous fate
Befalls them who us hate!
And hope we, through the coming days,
In Thee to glory—Thee to praise!

PART II.

Prayer in National Disaster.

O LORD, why cast us off,
Make us the nations' scoff?
For foes amid us rise,
And our just laws despise;
While thou dost not our hosts attend,
Nor from their enemies defend.

Our goods they make their prey,
Our men in battle slay.
We to distress are brought;
Thou sellest us for naught;
So that in our disgrace and shame,
The nations round despise our name!

Great are our sorrows, yet
We do not thee forget;

Nor from thy truth depart;
Nor draw from thee our heart;
Nor freedom's covenant forsake,
Which thou didst with our fathers make!

If we had turned from thee,
Or been from justice free,
Or made strange gods our own,
It all thou wouldst have known:
But as from thee we will not stay,
Our foes us slaughter all the day.

O Lord, for us awake!
Us into favor take;
While in the dust we lie,
Do not our suit deny;
But now our arms crown with success,
And us in thy great mercy bless.

PSALM XLV.

PART I.

Christ, the Glorious King.

OF thee, O Christ, I love to sing;
Thou art my Saviour and my King;
Loosen my tongue to sing thy praise,
And teach thy sacred laws and ways.

Fairer than all the sons of men
Thou art, and hast for ever been.
Great grace upon thy lips is poured—
For ever blessed, thou art the Lord.

Gird on thy sword, thy mighty power;
Make this a grand, successful hour;
For goodness, truth, and justice' sake,
Victorious power now to thee take.

Ride forth to conquest, Saviour, ride!
For thy right hand shall be thy guide.
Let all the nations fall before
Thy throne, and solemnly adore.

The throne supreme belongs to thee,
Thy scepter rules in equity;
All virtues are by thee possessed,
Of God above thy fellows blessed.

Perfume thy garments sweetly scents;
Thy praise pours forth from instruments;
The Church, thy bride, at thy right hand
Doth in her grace and beauty stand.

PART II.

The Church the Lamb's Bride.

O DAUGHTER of the Highest, hear,
And to thy Lord incline thine ear;

Forget thou not thy humble race,
Who have not yet been saved by grace!

If thou to Christ art ever true,
He then will thee with pleasure view;
Of thee the rich will favors seek,
And all of thy vast merits speak.

O thou art glorious to behold!
Thy robes embroidered are with gold!
And higher thou shalt yet ascend,
While joyful angels thee attend.

These shall with songs all join to sing,
Come to the palace of thy King!
Thy children then shall with thee stand,
All honored in that better land!

Thy name shall then be known abroad,
Through all the vast domains of God!
And all who do thy Lord adore,
Shall speak thy praise for evermore!

PSALM XLVI.
Security of the Church.

THE Lord is our refuge and strength;
  In trouble our help ever near;
The ground may be shaken beneath,
  But nothing the saints have to fear.

Though the waters of oceans should roar,
   And earth with their violence shake,
Or the mountains be hurled in the sea,
   God would not his people forsake!

He is in the midst of his Church,
   And cheers it with streams of his grace;
With him for its help and defense,
   It shall not be moved from its place.

Around it the nations all raged;
   But God by his voice drove them hence,
And kindly with us still remained—
   Our refuge, and strength, and defense!

Come, see all his works on the earth
   Which he has performed for our sake!
For us he makes wars rage or cease—
   His voice makes the nations to quake:

"Desist ye, and know I am God!
   I over the nations will reign;
My power shall extend through the earth
   And forever and ever remain!"

Around us the nations may rage,
   But God will soon drive them all hence;
And kindly with us still remain,
   Our refuge, and shield, and defense!

PSALM XLVII.

Exhortation to praise the Ascended Saviour.

O CLAP your hands, ye nations,
   And sing Jehovah's praise!
For on the earth he triumphs,
   And holy are his ways.

He is our king and Saviour,
   All others far above;
Our lot for us he's chosen,
   And placed on us his love!

He has to heaven ascended—
   'He is the mighty King!
Sing praise to him, sing praises!
   With joyful voices sing!

Sing to the risen Saviour!
   O sing his worthy praise!
He'll reign o'er all the nations
   Through all succeeding days.

The throne is his forever;
   His is a royal race;
The princes to him gather,
   All ransomed by his grace.

To Christ belong the mighty;
  His mercy they implore:
Supremely he's exalted—
  Let us his name adore!

PSALM XLVIII.

The Beauty and Security of Zion.

GREAT is Jehovah, the Sov'reign eternal;
  Greatly his praise should be sounded abroad;
Praise him, ye righteous, in his holy mountain,
  City established and chosen of God.

Beautiful is Zion in its elevation,
  Joy of the earth, ever peaceful and fair;
People from far gladly come to this temple—
  Refuge in danger, and hope in despair.

Earth's mighty ones all against it assemble;
  Schemes to destroy it ingeniously lay;
But as they gaze they are wholly confounded:
  Make it their refuge, or haste far away.

As we have heard, so we gladly have witnessed;
  Efforts of foes are all futile and vain;
God's holy city his strength has made mighty;
  Firm in his wisdom it e'er shall remain.

Think, O ye people, of his loving-kindness;
  Through all the earth declare ye his praise;
Justly he sways o'er the earth now his scepter,
  Hence all the righteous rejoice in his ways.

Go ye round Zion, and number her towers!
  Mark ye her bulwarks and palaces well!
Publish its strength to the next generation—
  God with his people for ever will dwell.

PSALM XLIX.

Death the Sure Fate of All.

THE PRELUDE.

COME all who understanding seek,
  To whate'er caste ye may belong;
My mouth shall words of wisdom speak—
  I'll utter truth in sacred song.

THE HYMN.

In evil days why should I fear,
  Encompassed by insidious foes,
They who in costly robes appear,
  And proudly in their wealth repose?

No man his brother can redeem
  That he on earth should ever live;

Too great is the demand for him—
    He has not the vast sum to give.

Alike the wise and foolish die,
    And all their worldly wealth forsake;
Even their houses, should they try,
    They could not undecaying make.

Their very names will soon decay,
    Though they in life for honor strove;
Their's was a vain and foolish way,
    And yet the world their lives approve.

Thus they descend into the grave,
    And no more have on earth a place;
Them God from death declined to save—
    But we for life will trust his grace.

Let fear nor envy thee distress
    When men around in wealth increase;
For death will them ere long possess,
    And then their glory all will cease.

Though thee all worldly men should praise,
    When for thyself thou doest well,
Thou soon shalt perish in thy ways,
    And ever cease on earth to dwell.

PSALM L.

PART I.

God Speaking in his Sanctuary.

THE mighty God calls to the earth
    From morning until night;
From Zion, beautiful and pure,
    Sends forth his holy light.

He comes in glorious majesty,
    And utters words profound;
Before him is devouring fire,
    And tempests rage around.

He comes and will his people judge,
    Who solemn vows have made;
"Now let them all," he cries aloud,
    "Before me be arrayed!"

His justice and his righteousness
    His works proclaim abroad;
On him the wise cannot impose:
    The judge is even God.

PART II.

God's Demand of his People.

HEAR, O my people! I will speak,
    And admonition give;

For I am God, thy God and King,
  By whom alone ye live.

For all thy sacrifices, brought
  Without sincerest love,
And works of righteousness and peace,
  I now will thee reprove.

The cattle on a thousand hills,
  And all the beasts, are mine;
And if thy heart is not sincere,
  I naught will have of thine.

With perfect vision, I the birds
  Of all the mountains see;
And did I need their sacrifice,
  I would not come to thee.

But with thanksgiving on thy lips,
  Come thou my throne before;
And pay thy vows to the Most High,
  And solemnly adore.

Then offer up thy fervent prayers
  When danger thee is nigh,
And I will thee defend; and thus
  Thou me shalt glorify.

PART III.

God's Demand of the Wicked.

THOU who dost live in wickedness,
    Why of my statutes speak?
Why my laws sound abroad, when thou
    Instruction dost not seek?

My words thou dost behind thee cast,
    To robbery consent;
In fellowship join with the vile,
    And speak with ill intent.

All these things often thou hast done,
    While silent I remained;
Till thou didst think I was like thee,
    And justice merely feigned.

But I at last will thee reprove,
    Will thy whole life inspect.
Stop! lest I thee in pieces tear,
    And no one thee protect.

But turn to me with heart sincere,
    And thou my grace shalt know;
For to him who regards his ways
    I will salvation show.

PSALM LI.

Confession and Prayer of a Penitent.

ACCORDING to thy mercy great,
O Lord, regard my wretched state;
In kindness all my sins forgive,
And let me by thy favor live.

Wash me from every sinful stain;
May no guilt on my heart remain;
For I my sins to thee confess—
They fill my heart with deep distress.

Against thee, Saviour, only thee,
My crimes were wrought, which now I see;
And me shouldst thou far from thee thrust,
Thou wouldst be righteous still, and just.

O'er my depravity I grieve,
For inborn sin doth to me cleave;
But thou canst wash the stain away,
And help me thy just laws obey.

O let me hear thy pard'ning voice!
Bid my poor, broken heart rejoice!
Yea, a clean heart in me create,
And me in saving grace instate.

Cast me not from thee, Lord, I pray;
Nor thy good Spirit take away:
May I thy great salvation gain;
And let thy Spirit me sustain.

Then will I teach thy holy ways,
And sinners, saved, shall learn thy praise;
Lord, now to me salvation bring,
And loud my tongue thy praise shall sing!

Hadst thou desired sacrifice,
It I had brought, of richest price;
But thee a contrite heart I give,
And it just now thou dost receive!

How sweet I find the gracious way!
And now for Zion, Lord, I pray;
Build up its walls, accept its praise—
Thy saints make joyful all their days.

PSALM LII.

The Deceitful Tongue.

O WHY in mischief take delight,
  Thou man of violence?
For God his goodness will maintain,
  And favors still dispense.

Thy tongue, which like a razor sharp,
　　Works mischief all the day;
Is a performer of deceit—
　　It speaks but to betray.

Thou tongue (the servant of a heart
　　Which grace has not renewed)
Thou lovest lying more than truth,
　　And evil more than good.

Thou ruin ever dost devise,
　　Alike of old and young;
Thou lovest all devouring words,
　　O thou deceitful tongue!

But thou art to destruction doomed;
　　Soon run is thy short race;
God thee will seize, and as is just,
　　Tear from thy dwelling-place.

The righteous shall behold and fear;
　　Proclaim his fall abroad
Who trusted in deceit and wealth,
　　But sought not help from God.

But they, like the green olive trees,
　　Shall in God's temple stand;
Shall in his gracious works rejoice,
　　And prosper in the land.

PSALM LIII.

Universal Depravity.

SAYS the heart of the foolish ones, "There is
    no God!"
  They all are corrupt and have hateful things
    done;
Though great is their number, not one doeth
    good;
  God looked down from heaven, and he could
    find none.

None fully their duty to God understand,
  But all with delight into wickedness run;
Our race now is fallen throughout all the land,
  There is none that good doeth; no, not even
    one.

But shall not all they who in sin take delight,
  Who, hating God's people, them fiercely
    devour,
And shunning his worship, bow not in his
    sight,
  Be judged in the end, and feel his dread
    power?

Ah! then shall they tremble before him in fear;
　But the righteous he will more abundantly bless;
For though they now meet with derision and sneer,
　Their refuge he stands in the day of distress.

O that out of Zion salvation would come
　To them thou didst ransom, the race of thy choice!
When thine exiles on earth thou at last shalt bring home,
　They then shall praise thee, and in gladness rejoice.

PSALM LIV.

Prayer and Praise.

O SAVE me by thy name,
　My God, my Strength, my Friend!
Now let my prayer before thee come,
　Do thou my cause defend.

For foes against me rise;
　Oppressors seek my life;
They set not Thee before their eyes,
　But take delight in strife.

Behold! God is my help;
　He will my life preserve;
But them cut off, for his truth's sake,
　Who him refuse to serve.

To thee I sacrifice,
　My God, my Strength, my Friend!
I offer joyful songs of praise,
　For thou dost me defend.

PSALM LV.

Prayer for Deliverance from Enemies.

HEAR, O God, my supplication,
　Listen to my earnest prayer;
All day long do I go mourning,
　For my foes would me ensnare.
My heart trembles in my bosom
　At the sight of danger near!
Death's dread terrors all have seized me!
　I am overwhelmed by fear!

O how oft I, in my sorrow,
　Think, had I wings like a dove,
I would fly to peaceful regions,
　And there find the rest I love!

I would haste away for shelter,
  From the fearful, rushing wind;
I would thus escape from sorrow—
  Quiet and contentment find.

Ah! not foes alone revile me;
  I such sorrow could have borne;
Were I hated by a stranger,
  I would have less cause to mourn:
But my friend and mine acquaintance,
  With whom I sweet counsel held,
He who joined with me in worship,
  Has against my life rebelled.

Thus I am by foes surrounded,
  Who do not delight in peace;
Lord, I pray, divide their counsels!
  Let fraud and oppression cease!
Wickedness is in their dwellings;
  Still thou me wilt from them save;
Suddenly shall death seize on them—
  They shall sink into the grave.

I at morn, and noon, and evening,
  Will to thee lift up my voice,
For thou present art to save me,
  That my heart may yet rejoice.

As they had escaped reverses,
   They rebelled against their friend;
All their words were false, deceitful;
   But thou wilt the just defend.

PSALM LVI.

Confidence in God's Care.

HAVE pity on me, O my God,
   For men pant for my life;
Through all the day they me oppress,
   And take delight in strife.
But though my foes against me join,
   Still will I trust in thee;
God is my friend; I will not fear;
   What can flesh do to me?

Against me evil they devise,
   And all my words misstate;
Together do they watch my steps,
   And for me lie in wait.
But shall they by deceit prevail?
   In mercy on me look!
Are not my tears by thee preserved,
   And written in thy book?

My enemies turn back dismayed,
   When, Lord, I cry to thee;

God is my friend; I will not fear;
    What can flesh do to me?
Thy promises to me are sure,
    And now thy name I praise;
For thou hast me preserved from death,
    And lengthened out my days.

PSALM LVII.

Our Safety is in God.

TO me be merciful, O God;
    Myself I on thy goodness cast—
Rest in the shadow of thy wings,
    Till life's calamities are past.
I call upon the Lord most high:
    He will from heaven salvation send,
And put to shame my enemies,
    And me in love and truth defend.

My foes are as the beasts of prey,
    And for my life they lie in wait;
Nay, they as fiends do breathe out fire,
    Eager to bring me to my fate!
Their teeth are spears, their tongues a sword—
    O God, protect me in thy ways!
Thy name above the heavens exalt!
    Above the earth thy ceaseless praise!

A net they in my pathway spread—
  But by it were themselves ensnared:
A pit they digged me to engulf—
  Their fate was that for me prepared!
My heart is strengthened, O my God;
  I'll make in song thy mercies known;
Awake, my soul! My harp, awake!
  I will awake with early dawn.

Among the nations thee I'll praise;
  Among the kingdoms joyful sing;
Thy mercy reaches to the heavens,
  Thy truth, the clouds, eternal King!
Thy name above the heavens exalt!
  Above the earth thy ceaseless praise!
Then will I put in thee my trust
  And ever walk in wisdom's ways.

PSALM LVIII.

An Invective against the Wicked.

JUDGE ye uprightly, mighty ones?
  Deal justice with an even hand?
Nay, ye iniquity devise,
  And weigh out violence in the land.

The wicked are from birth estranged;
  Sin's deadly poison in them reigns;

They, like deaf adders, will not hear
  Truth's holy and enchanting strains.

Break thou their teeth, O righteous Lord!
  May they as water waste away;
Defeat their aims; and may their schemes,
  Abortive, never see the day!

The sudden whirlwind on them bring!
  Then shall all they who in thee trust,
Declare, "Reward is for the good—
  The Judge of all the earth is just."

PSALM LIX.

God Trusted in Danger.

DEFEND me from my foes, O God;
And save me from the men of blood,
Who unprovoked against me rise,
And mischief in their hearts devise.
To judge the nations, Lord, awake!
And to thee power and vengeance take.
Let mercy not by them be found,
Who lie in siege the city round.
Their mouths belch forth malicious words,
Which on their lips are piercing swords!
They boasting say, "Who will us hear,
Whom we have any cause to fear!"

But thou their words need'st not be told;
Thou dost them in derision hold.
On thee, my Strength, my hope is stayed;
Grant me in mercy now thine aid.

Lest we forget, do not them slay,
But by thy power drive them away;
Come thou upon them in their pride,
Whose sinful lips have cursed and lied:
Consume them till there none remains,
That we may know Jehovah reigns.
Or let them, quite cut off from good,
Howl in their fruitless search for food;
While saved by thee, Eternal King,
I of thy power and mercy sing.
Thou art my refuge in distress;
Thou dost me with thy favor bless.
On thee, my Strength, my hope is stayed;
Grant me in mercy now thine aid.

PSALM LX.

Prayer in National Distress.

O GOD, thou hast forsaken us,
   And in thy wrath cast down;
Our land is by its troubles rent,
   And trembles 'neath thy frown.

Wilt thou not us revive again?
  Our land's sad breaches heal?
For thou hast made us see distress—
  With wine of wrath to reel.

For thy truth's sake a banner give
  Which over us shall wave;
That we may from our foes escape,
  Extend thy hand to save.

Thy promises rejoice my heart;
  On them my hope I stay;
The tribes around shall to me yield,
  And own my rightful sway.

Who will me lead against my foes?
  Bring to the city strong?
Wilt thou not, who didst us forsake,
  For deeds unjust and wrong?

O aid thou us in our distress,
  For help of man is vain!
Through thee we shall do valiantly,
  And soon the vict'ry gain.

PSALM LXI.

The Exile's Return.

O GOD, great in mercy, attend to my prayer,
  For now from afar unto thee do I cry;

In sorrow of heart, overwhelmed by despair,
  Lead me to the Rock that is higher than I.

From the Eden of innocence far gone astray,
  In exile I wander in want and distress;
But now to my Refuge I speed me away—
  Christ waits to receive me, to comfort and bless.

My foe rises up, and me fiercely assails,
  Lest I should in Christ find protection and rest;
But grace in my rescue and safety prevails;
  I now with the Lord for my portion am blest.

Henceforth will I seek the fair temple above;
  I journey my Lord and Redeemer to see;
While o'er me extends the broad wings of his love,
  To guard me until I from danger am free.

For ever my life there my Lord will prolong,
  That with him enthroned evermore I may reign,
To sing all enraptured redemption's sweet song,
  Now free from temptation, and sorrow, and pain.

PSALM LXII.

Christ our Refuge.

HOW long will foes assault me,
    And think to cast me down?
While Satan speaks of blessing,
    He doth upon me frown.

On Christ my soul reposes,
    He will salvation give;
He is the Rock of Refuge;
    In him I hope to live.

Christ is my help and glory,
    My Rock for ever strong;
O trust him, all ye people,
    And to your Refuge throng.
        On Christ my soul, etc.

Place all men in the balance,
    And thus their merit try;
It in the meek is nothing,
    And in the proud a lie.
        On Christ my soul, etc.

Trust not in your possessions,
    Nor merit seek to gain;

If good works are your riches,
   Let not your heart be vain.
       On Christ my soul, etc.

To Christ belongs all power
   To judge or pardon sin;
And he at last will render
   Each as his work has been.
       On Christ my soul, etc.

PSALM LXIII.

Fervent Aspirations after God.

MY soul now thirsts, O God, for thee;
   While in a world of doubt and shade,
I would thy power and glory see,
   As they are in thy house displayed.

Thy love is better far than life;
   It my most fervent praise demands;
And joyful 'mid this state of strife,
   I in thy name lift up my hands.

Yea, the rich bounties of thy grace
   My longing soul shall satisfy:
Then from my lips unceasing praise,
   Like incense, shall ascend on high.

I call to mind, in night's lone hour,
   Thy countless mercies in the past;
And then for safety trust thy power,
   And all my cares upon thee cast.

Fain in the shadow of thy wings
   Now find I safety and repose;
And while to thee my spirit clings,
   Thou wilt not yield me to my foes.

Me for my piety they hate,
   And even would destroy my soul;
But they shall meet a wretched fate—
   Soon death o'er them shall have control.

But I will still rejoice in thee,
   With them who on thy name rely;
While error from the land shall flee,
   And truth stand guarded from on high.

PSALM LXIV.

Prayer for Protection.

HEAR me, O Lord, now while I pray!
   Save from the cruel foe;
Hide me secure from wicked men,
   Who brawling round me go.
Their tongues they make like piercing swords;
Like arrows shoot their poisoned words.

In secret they shoot at the just;
  Them to destroy agree;
They cautiously arrange their snares,
  And say, "Who can them see?"
They their intentions closely keep;
Each heart is an unfathomed deep.

God will an arrow at them shoot—
  Inflict a sudden wound;
And their own tongues shall them betray—
  Soon they shall not be found.
The wicked then in awe shall stand;
The righteous triumph in the land.

PSALM LXV.

The God of Grace and Nature Praised.

PRAISE waits in Zion, Lord, for thee;
  Thy saints draw near their vows to pay;
And all, ere long, shall bow the knee
  To Him who hears us when we pray.

Thy holy laws have we transgressed,
  But thou our sins wilt purge away;
And he is more than others blessed,
  Who in thy temple spends this day.

For here shall we be satisfied
  With bounties rich of saving grace;

And no good thing shall be denied
   Him who devoutly seeks thy face.

Thy righteous judgments thou dost send
   In answer to believing prayer;
Hence on thee now mankind attend,
   And place their confidence and care.

The mountains by thy power stand fast,
   The sea's loud roar is stilled by thee;
The tumults of the people last
   No longer than thou dost decree!

Before thee all the nations stand,
   And trembling view thy righteous ways;
While morn and eve, through every land,
   Rejoicing, sing thy worthy praise.

The earth thou visitest with rain,
   Thus making soft the furrowed fields;
Thou blessest, too, the shooting grain,
   So that the ground abundance yields.

Thy goodness crowns the passing year,
   The little hills are joyous things,
The valleys all rich clothing wear,
   And nature in thy presence sings.

PSALM LXVI.

PART I.

A National Hymn of Praise.

YE lands, adore the name of God!
　Make glorious his praise;
To honor him, proclaim aloud,
　"How wonderful his ways!"

Thy foes thou, by thy mighty power,
　Dost to submission bring;
Hence all the world should thee adore,
　And to thee joyful sing.

Great works God 'mid the nations wrought,
　The sea turned to dry land;
And led his people through the deep,
　By his almighty hand.

God reigns for ever on the earth;
　Toward him, ye nations, gaze;
Do not yourselves o'er him exalt,
　Nor weak rebellion raise.

But, yielding to his sov'reign sway,
　Proclaim aloud his praise;
For he it is preserves your lives,
　And guides you in his ways.

Though us he as the silver tried,
   And sorrows on us laid,
He us delivered by his power,
   And strong and wealthy made.

PART II.

Religious Experience Told.

I TO thy house, O God, will come,
   And my vows to thee pay,
Which solemnly my lips pronounced
   In trouble's gloomy day.

Come now, all ye who fear the Lord,
   And hearken every one,
While in your presence I relate
   What God for me has done.

I called upon him in distress,
   And he received my prayer;
My sins forgave, made glad my heart—
   I felt no burden there.

And now his praise is on my tongue,
   His Spirit in my heart;
And I would not, for sinful joys,
   From Christ, my Lord, depart.

Thus surely God inclined his ear,
   And heard my plaintive voice;
Blessed be the Saviour's precious name!
   I in his love rejoice.

PSALM LXVII.

A Hymn of Praise.

TO us, O Lord, incline,
   And us thy people own;
O cause on us thy face to shine,
   And make thy glory known!

Thine is the power to save;
   By thee the nations live;
At first thou their existence gave,
   Now their glad praise receive.

O'er kingdoms thou dost reign;
   Their fate thy scepter sways;
May they thy subjects e'er remain,
   And thee devoutly praise.

Beneath thy fruitful smile
   The earth its increase yields;
And great is our rejoicing, while
   Thou blessest all our fields.

Grant us thy blessing still;
  Our praise be pleased to hear;
Thy purposes on earth fulfill,
  And keep us in thy fear.

PSALM LXVIII.

The God of Israel with his People.

LET God in majesty arise!
His foes disperse before his eyes.
As melts the wax before the fire,
Before him the unjust expire;
While all the righteous raise their voice,
And in his presence fain rejoice.

Now sing to him your joyous lay,
And through the desert make your way;
For, lo! he rides in glory forth,
The God and Ruler of the earth,
The Father of the fatherless,
The widow's Friend in her distress.
Forsaken ones before him stand,
And dwell in houses in the land;
He comes to liberate the bound,
And for them scatter blessings round;
But the rebellious to disperse
With leanness and affliction curse!

O God, thou didst thy saints defend,
And through the wilderness attend.
Before thy presence quaked the earth;
The heavens poured their bounties forth;
Bold Sinai thy voice did hear,
And trembled with excessive fear.
Thy people strength from thee received,
When, worn with toil, afflicted, grieved,
They by the guidance of thy hand
Themselves established in the land,
Which thou didst to the needy give
That there they might securely live;
And made them triumph o'er the strong,
When virgin minstrels sang this song:
"The kings and armies far have fled;
Our matrons on their riches fed;
And now securely they repose,
Unterrified by cruel foes;
Richly attired, fair to behold,
Like wings of doves, o'erspread with gold.
When God reached forth his vengeful hand,
With bones was whitened all the land."

And now ye hills of Bashan, why
With Zion proudly think to vie?
Why in your pride do ye look down
On that God doth with glory crown?

Where he, while all his saints adore,
Resides, and will for evermore?
His chariots on him attend;
And myriads from heaven descend
To Zion's holy, sacred place,
Where he bestows his gifts of grace;
As when on Sinai he came,
And made its lofty summit flame.

God has gone up to Zion's hill,
His purposes there to fulfill;
He has the vanquished captive led,
And gifts received, and conquests made.
'Mid the rebellious he will dwell,
And guard his chosen people well.
The Lord be praised by us each day,
Who takes our burdens all away:
He ever present is to save
From sudden death—the yawning grave;
While in his wrath he smites the head
Of those a wicked life have led:
And says, "I will hurl back the foes
Who rise my people to oppose.
Red shall thy foot be where they stood—
Even thy dogs shall drink their blood!"

We saw the grand procession move
To Zion's hill, which thou dost love.

Before went forth the singers fain,
The minstrels followed in the train;
While in the midst, richly arrayed,
The damsels on their timbrels played.
They who from Israel's fountain came,
Praise offer to Jehovah's name;
From Benjamin's to Judah's band,
They come on Zion's hill to stand.

For Israel God strength ordained;
He has his people's rights maintained.
O Lord, kings shall, thy house to see,
Come, and rich presents bring to thee.
Rebuke the brutish men of war;
The heathen whom thou dost abhor;
Let them to thee their silver bring,
And own thou art th' Almighty King.
Ye kingdoms, sing Jehovah's praise!
He glorious is in all his ways;
Upon the ancient heavens he rides,
His voice the cloudy sky divides;
It rolls in majesty along—
He is the Lord for ever strong;
Strength from his sanctuary sends,
His people faithfully defends;
He them endows with strength and power;
Praise ye the Lord for evermore!

PSALM LXIX.

PART I.

Persecution of the Righteous.

THE waves of sorrow o'er me flow,
    Into my life the waters press;
I sink down deep into the mire;
    O save me, Lord, in my distress!
Mine eyes are wasted by my grief,
    I'm faint while I thy help implore;
For without cause men are my foes;
    What I took not I must restore!

But thou dost my offenses know;
    O let not them be put to shame,
Who through me thy salvation sought,
    And trusted in thy holy name!
I for thy sake endure reproach;
    Estranged become my nearest friends;
Zeal for thy house has me consumed;
    Thy foes my righteousness offends.

When I wear sackcloth, weep and fast,
    Reproach attends me all day long;
The beggars at the gates revile,
    And driv'ling sots make me their song.

Yet, Lord, I prayer address to thee;
　Accept my offerings in love;
Me graciously thy help afford,
　And from the waves and mire remove.

PART II.

God our Support in Persecution.

HEAR me, O Lord, in thy great love;
　Thy face no longer from me hide;
Draw me to thee from my distress,
　That I securely may abide.
Thou knowest my unjust reproach,
　Which breaks my heart, and makes me moan;
Here no true comforters I find;
　I look for pity; there is none!

To me for food they offer gall;
　They vinegar give in my thirst;
To them their tables make a snare;
　Let them be in thy justice cursed:
For whom thou smitest they deride,
　And find strange pleasure in their pain;
Add to them punishment of sin,
　Nor let them with the just remain.

But from the deep set me on high;
　My praise then for thy saving aid

Shall to thee far more grateful be
  Than beasts upon thine altar laid.
This seen, the sorrowing shall rejoice;
  Let heaven and earth thy glories tell;
Save Zion, and our cities build;
  May those who love thee in them dwell.

PSALM LXX.

Prayer in Temptation.

HASTE, O God, my soul to save,
Lest I sink below the grave;
Hast thou not atonement made?
Quickly come unto mine aid.

May my constant, subtile foe,
Who would me involve in woe,
And my very life devour,
Be defeated by thy power.

Be the tempter driven back,
As he comes me to attack;
But may all the saints rejoice—
In thy praise employ their voice.

Though I am a suff'rer here,
To my cry God turns his ear;
Come, my Saviour, now, I pray;
Me to bless make no delay.

PSALM LXXI.

Prayer for Assistance in Old Age.

LORD, I put my trust in thee,
    Divert the ills I fear;
In thy goodness rescue me
    From every danger near.
Hearken to my earnest prayer;
    Be thou the Rock of my abode;
For I make my refuge there—
    I trust in thee, my God.

Thou hast blessed me in the past,
    And still thou art my hope;
Shall the hand of the unjust
    Be proudly lifted up?
O, my Saviour, rescue me!
    To thee I rightfully belong;
From my youth I trusted thee,
    And thou hast been my song.

Many wonder that I stand
    Securely in distress;
But my refuge is thy hand,
    Strong both to save and bless.
Thou my mouth hast filled with praise;
    Cast me not off when I am old;

But protect me all my days,
    And in thine arms enfold.

Enemies arise who say,
    "God now is not his friend;
We will him pursue and slay;
    For none will him defend!"
But be thou not far from me;
    My confidence is thy great name;
Let them all dishonored be,
    And clothed in lasting shame.

Hope, which gives strength to the weak,
    I joyfully possess;
And will of thy goodness speak—
    Thy mercies numberless.
Making known thy works and truth,
    Thus far have I pursued my way;
Thou hast taught me from my youth;
    When old, cast not away.

I would still proclaim thy power,
    For who is like to thee?
Thou didst send a troubled hour,
    That we our sins might see:
But thou wilt us bless again,
    I shall with harp thy mercies sing;
Thou wilt still my friend remain—
    My foes to shame wilt bring.

PSALM LXXII.

The Triumphant Reign of Christ.

JESUS, immortal King, to thee
    Justice and righteousness belong;
Thou governest in equity,
    Opposed to violence and wrong.

The mountains of thy guarding power,
    Give to thy people constant peace;
For them, while sun and moon endure,
    Thy watchful care shall never cease.

Like gentle showers upon the earth,
    Thy fruitful grace on them descends;
And as they in thy ways go forth,
    It them along their course attends.

Thy kingdom is from sea to sea;
    Upon the earth it has no bounds;
Before thee all shall bow the knee—
    Success thy every effort crowns.

Yea, kings themselves before thee fall,
    And princes thee delight to serve;
The poor thou hearest when they call;
    The weak thou dost divinely nerve,

The artless guardest from deceit,
  From violence the friendless one:
Their gold all lands cast at thy feet;
  By thee amazing works are done.

Thee ceaseless prayer the saints address,
  And joyful sing thy worthy praise;
Abundant grace do they possess,
  And flourish hence in wisdom's ways.

Thy kingdom evermore shall stand,
  Long as the sun thy name endure;
Thou shalt be praised in every land;
  Thy saints are in thy grace secure.

Doxology.

PRAISED be the God of Israel,
  He wond'rous works for us has done;
Praise ye his name, his glories tell—
  The great, eternal, triune One!

BOOK III.

PSALM LXXIII.

PART I.

The Portion of the Wicked in this Life.

GOD to the pure in heart is good,
   Yet I almost renounced his law;
For I was envious of the proud,
   When their prosperity I saw.

Even in death they oft escape
   The pains which other men endure;
While blessings, numberless and free,
   Through life their happiness insure.

Hence pride they as a collar wear,
   And clothe themselves in violence;
Around they impudently stare,
   And boldly tell their vile intents.

Their words are haughty through conceit,
   While they oppression vindicate;
Their mouth against the heavens they set,
   And through the earth they proudly prate:

"How doth God know our thoughts and
    ways?
  With the Most High is knowledge
    found?"
Behold these are ungodly men,
  Who on the earth in wealth abound.

I verily have cleansed my heart,
  And washed from guilt my hands, in
    vain;
For all day long have I been plagued,
  And every morning scourged with pain.

Should I the wicked imitate,
  I would God's people thus betray;
But these thoughts tended to perplex;
  My mind was pained by this survey.

Then to God's temple I repaired,
  And there foresaw their coming fate;
Ah, they in slippery places stand,
  And fearful judgments them await!

They in a moment are cast down,
  And by consuming woes surprised;
As is a dream when one awakes,
  Their vain show is by God despised.

PART II.

God the Christian's Portion.

WHEN vexed by the prosperity
   On earth by wicked men enjoyed,
O Lord, the truth I did not see,
   But stupidly myself annoyed.

I now know thou art by my side,
   And dost not me a moment leave;
Thou wilt through life unerring guide,
   And then to glory me receive.

O, whom in heaven have I but thee?
   Or whom on earth so much desire?
Though my heart fail, and comforts flee,
   With strength thou wilt my heart inspire.

Thou ever wilt my portion be,
   And give me endless peace and joy;
But all who are estranged from thee,
   Thou wilt for evermore destroy.

And now with profit I draw near
   To thee, O Lord, in earnest prayer;
Yea, I have learned to trust thee here,
   And would to all thy works declare.

PSALM LXXIV.
Prayer for the Church in Persecution.

WHY, O our God, us forever abandon?
   Why in thine anger thy people consume?
Us thou didst purchase to be thy possession;
   Think of us kindly, thy mercy resume.

Haste thou thy coming to our desolations,
   Visit Mount Zion, where once thou didst dwell;
Foes have abused every thing in thy temple;
   Where once we met, now their triumphs they tell.

Here they their symbols for signs have erected,
   Broken its altars, its beauty defaced;
Fire have they cast into thy habitation,
   By wicked rites it profaned and disgraced.

Yea, they have burned all our houses of worship,
   Left us no signs still our hearts to assure;
While in the land there is nowhere a prophet,
   Telling how long we these woes shall endure.

How long, O God? for thine eye scans the future;
   Ever shall foes thus blaspheme and annoy?

Why thou thy right hand from them still
    withdrawest?
Take from thy bosom, and bid it destroy.

Thou, as our King, didst of old work salvation;
    Naught from thy power was able to fly;
Rocks in thy presence poured forth streams of
    water,
    While mighty rivers themselves became dry.

Both day and night hast thou at thy disposal;
    Thou didst the sun's light and glory decree;
Earth thou established in all its extension;
    Summer and winter were ordered by thee.

But in the land are the vile and ungodly;
    By them Jehovah is mocked and reviled;
O Lord, remember in mercy thy people;
    Thy turtle-dove save from the wicked and
        wild.

Think of thy covenant in our affliction,
    Then shall thy people again praise thy name:
And although cruelty has its dark places,
    They who trust thee shall be strangers to
        shame.

Daily the impious, O Lord, revile thee;
  Daily they murmur against thy just laws;
Hear how the noise of their clamor increases—
  Rise! and in majesty maintain thy cause.

PSALM LXXV.

God Reigns over the Nations.

NEAR is thy name, O God;
  Our thanks to thee we give;
We will thy wondrous works declare,
  And these thy words receive:
"I judge in equity,
  As things to me unfold;
And while commotion fills the world,
  Its pillars I uphold."

Lord, I the vile rebuke;
  The proud I bid be meek,
Nor boldly stand with lofty head,
  Nor confidently speak.
Promotion is from God,
  Vain is ambitious hope,
For he from power puts down one,
  And sets another up.

The cup of wrath he holds,
  (Whate'er they do or think)

Is for the wicked; and its dregs
   They in their time shall drink.
Hence I will him extoll,
   Who says, while him I praise:
"I will the wicked thrust from power,
   To power the righteous raise!"

PSALM LXXVI.

Thanksgiving for Victory.

GREAT is the name of Israel's God,
In Judah published all abroad.
Mount Zion is his dwelling place,
Whence, in the fullness of his grace,
He broke the lightning of the bow—
All weapons which in war we know.
More glorious thou in Zion's hill,
Than mountains daring robbers fill.
The mighty were hurled to the ground;
They sank into their sleep profound.
Horsemen and chariots fell before
Thy dread rebuke, to rise no more.
O God, when thou dost judge the land,
Who can before thine anger stand?
Thou judgment didst from heaven reveal,
While the earth trembled and was still;

Appearing in thy majesty,
To set th' oppressed and captives free.
Man wrath God makes proclaim his praise,
And the remaining wrath allays.
Hence pay your vows to God, our King,
And to him gifts and off'rings bring.
He hurls down princes from the throne,
And reigns o'er all supreme alone.

PSALM LXXVII.
PART I.
Grief for the State of the Church.

I CALL on thee, O God, for help
   In trouble's gloomy day;
And in the night my hands lift up—
   From comfort turn away.

I think of thee in my distress;
   All night my vigils last;
I am so grieved I cannot speak
   When I think of the past.

I call to mind my songs at night,
   When we were greatly blessed;
Then, glancing o'er our present state,
   My spirit cannot rest.

Will God be angry evermore,
 And leave us thus destroyed?
Is mercy utterly withdrawn?
 And is his promise void?

Has God forgotten to be good?
 Us banished from his mind?
Or is it mine infirmity,
 A change in God to find?

I will remember all thy works,
 Which show how just thou art;
And talk about what thou hast done,
 To reassure my heart.

PART II.

The Deliverance of the Israelites.

THY ways are holy, O my God,
 None other is like thee;
Thou wond'rous works for us hast done,
 That men thy power may see.

With strong arm thou didst us redeem
 When dangers gathered near;
The waters saw thee in thy might,
 And were impressed with fear.

Yea, trembling seized the mighty deep,
 While loud the skies resound;

The clouds abundant waters poured;
Thine arrows flew around.

Thy thunders in the whirlwind roared!
Abroad the lightnings glared!
The earth beneath thy footsteps shook!
The sea thy way prepared!

Through th' great waters was thy path;
And by thy servant's hand
Thou didst thy people safely lead,
And give the promised land.

PSALM LXXVIII.

Admonition to keep God's Commandments.

O PEOPLE, to my words give ear,
And earnestly my teaching hear.
· I will speak words in sacred song
Which to the distant past belong.
The works our fathers have us told
We'll from our children not withhold;
But carefully to them make known
The wonders God for us has done.
He gave this law in Israel,
That we should our children tell,
And they to theirs, the works of old.
Which then our fathers did behold;

And that we in his care should trust,
Obey his law, be true and just;
And not like them from him depart,
And stubborn make our sinful heart;
And waver, and reject his grace,
Nor on him our reliance place.

Yet Ephraim's unstable tribe
Did not upon their hearts inscribe
God's holy laws, but seemed to be
Like bowmen who in battle flee.
They by their vows did not abide,
But from his statutes turned aside;
And from their yielding thoughts expelled
The wonders which their eyes beheld.
For deeds astounding, by his hand,
Were done in Egypt's distant land:
He did for them the sea divide,
And them across in safety guide:
He led them by a cloud by day,
And fire by night, through all their way:
He cleft the rock when they were dry,
And gave of water a supply.
Yet in the desert they complained,
Nor faithful to their God remained;
With him their heart they kept not right,
But asked for food for their delight;

And in their rude rebellion said,
"Can here God a rich table spread?
He smote the rock, and waters burst
Thence to allay our burning thirst;
But is he able to provide
Bread, that we all may be supplied?"

These words provoked Jehovah's ire,
Which raged as a devouring fire.
Their faith not being on him stayed,
They trusted not in him for aid;
Though he had swept the clouds aside,
Thrown the broad doors of heaven wide,
And rained down manna from the sky,
The corn of heaven—a rich supply;
The food which answers angels well—
And all ate of the bread that fell.
Then the south wind he caused to blow,
And rained flesh on the earth below;
Yea, feathered fowls he them sent down,
Which as the sand o'erspread the ground.
Thus their desire was not denied;
With flesh enough they were supplied;
But while their mouths were filled with food,
They murmured still against their God:
When he, their strong men striking down
Turn'd on them with indignant frown.

Yet they did not from sin desist,
Nor cease Jehovah to resist;
Hence he them to destruction doomed,
Their days to be for naught consumed.

Then they appeared to turn to God,
Subdued by his chastising rod;
Him as their Rock in prayer addressed,
And their Redeemer him confessed.
But even then they falsely spake,
And merely did pretension make;
For their hearts were not yet content,
Nor steadfast in his covenant.
Yet them he graciously forgave,
And interposed his power to save;
He put his anger all aside,
That they might still on earth abide;
For them he knew, how short they last,
A breath that comes not back when passed.

How oft their God they disobeyed
While in the wilderness they strayed!
In ways which one can scarcely tell,
Provoked the God of Israel.
They thought not of the mighty hand
That saved them from a hostile land;
What wonders God in Egypt wrought,
And how against their foes He fought.

He turned their rivers into blood,
And made unwholesome all their food;
He them by swarming flies annoyed,
Sent frogs among them which destroyed;
Their fruits to caterpillars gave,
Let locusts all their labor have;
Their vines and cattle gave to hail,
Let frosts their sycamores assail;
Sent thunderbolts their flocks to slay,
Fierce indignation, night and day;
Angels of evil, wrath, and woe,
Till they should let his people go:
Sent plague to putrefy their breath;
He spared them even not from death:
Till at the last, with vengeful hand,
He smote the first born of the land.

Then set he all his people free,
And safely guided through the sea;
Them in the dreary desert led,
And as they needed kindly fed;
While on their foes he brought the waves,
Made in the sea their restless graves.
But them brought to their land at last,
From thence for them the nations cast;
And gave each tribe its proper share,
That they might dwell securely there.

But even then they tempted God,
And were not by his presence awed;
They like their fathers him denied,
Turned like a treacherous bow aside;
High places to his courts preferred,
His jealousy by idols stirred,
Until his anger fiercely burned,
And Israel he greatly spurned;
So that from Shiloh, where on earth
He dwelt with men, he soon went forth;
His ark of strength gave to the foe,
A captive from its place to go;
His people to the cruel sword;
The land to be by fire devoured;
While death should their young men assail,
And maidens not their fate bewail;
And priests should by the sword be slain,
And still their widows not complain.

Yet from them long God could not keep,
But waked at last as one from sleep,
Or as a hero who had been
By wine o'ercome, passed by their sin,
And hurled their foes back to their place,
Clothed in confusion and disgrace.
Still he the tents of Joseph passed,
And Ephraim behind him cast,

And to the tribe of Judah came,
And there made glorious his name;
Erecting safe on Zion's hill
The temple he was pleased to fill;
And David chose, the shepherd youth,
With whom he found the love of truth,
And from the humble sheepfolds took,
To feed the people of his flock.
And he with singleness of heart,
Did words of truth to them impart;
He guided them with prudent skill,
And duty taught them to fulfill.

PSALM LXXIX.

A Hymn in Time of Great Persecution.

O GOD, our foes thy holy place
Enter, and it pollute, disgrace!
Thy Zion they in ruins lay,
Thy saints give to the birds a prey;
Their flesh to wild beasts of the earth,
And pour their blood as water forth:
And while we thus are bruised and torn,
Our neighbors look on us with scorn.

Lord, should thy jealousy still burn?
From us thy righteous anger turn!

But let thy wrath destructive fall
On them who do not on thee call.
For they are thy relentless foes,
And have on us brought countless woes:
Now for thy name's sake us forgive
And help us in thy fear to live.
Why should the foes around us say,
"Their God has cast them quite away!"
O Thou who art both just and good,
Soon let th' avenging of our blood,
Poured for our faith upon the ground,
Be manifest to all around.

Still longer shall the pris'ners sigh?
O listen to their mournful cry!
According to thy mighty power,
Save from our foes' appointed hour;
Give us not yet to death a prey,
But turn the threatened fate away.
May the reproach they cast on thee
Return, and their confusion be.
So shall thy people, all their days,
Thee for thy ceaseless mercies praise.

PSALM LXXX.

Israel compared to a Vine.

SHEPHERD of Israel, give ear;
Thou leader of thy people, hear;

Between the cherubim shine forth;
With brighter rays illume the earth;
With power omnipotent begirt,
Before the saints thy strength exert;
Light of thy countenance reveal,
Nor turn from our devout appeal.
Thou hast us given bread of tears;
Exposed us to our neighbors' jeers;
Do not from us thyself conceal,
Light of thy countenance reveal.

Thou didst a vine from Egypt bring,
O'er it thy kind protection fling,
For it a fruitful place prepare,
And plant it then securely there,
And reaching forth on every hand,
Its roots ran out and filled the land;
Its branches o'er the cedars spread;
It o'er the mountain cast its shade;
Its boughs sent out far to the sea,
And to the river, glad and free.
Why hast thou turned on it thy frown,
And all its hedges broken down?
That all who pass on it should feast,
Exposed to every hungry beast!
O God of hosts, we thee beseech;
Thine ear may our petition reach;

Look down from heaven, to us incline,
O have regard now to this vine!
Protect that planted by thy hand,
And made strong by thee in the land—
Ah! 'tis cut down and burn'd with fire!
Destroyed by thy consuming ire!

Still may thy watchful care be o'er
The Man thy hand has placed in power;
Then into sin we shall not fall,
But on thy name devoutly call.
Appear, and our backslidings heal—
Light of thy countenance reveal.

PSALM LXXXI.

God's Admonition to his People.

THE PRELUDE.

SING joyfully to God, our strength;
  Raise now a thankful song;
With timbrel and sweet-sounding harp
  His worthy praise prolong.
The new and full moon trumpets blow,
  Proclaim each festal day;
This law God 'gave, when us he led
  From Egypt safe away.

THE HYMN.

When thou wast in the bonds of sin,
    Employed in drudgery,
I heard thy plaintive, earnest prayer,
    And kindly set thee free.

To prove thee, and increase thy strength,
    I thee afflictions gave;
Waters of bitterness and strife;
    But present was to save.

Hear thou my admonition now;
    Have no strange god with thee,
For I alone am the Supreme;
    Hence worship only Me.

From bondage did I bring thee forth,
    And save in other days;
Now open in my house thy mouth,
    And it I'll fill with praise.

Be not like ancient Israel,
    Who would not me obey,
So that I left them to themselves,
    To walk in sorrow's way.

But ever hearken thou to me,
    And I will be thy guide;
I will thine enemies subdue—
    Turn coming ills aside.

I'll grant thee great prosperity;
The bread of heaven I'll give,
The wheat and honey of my house;
And thou with me shalt live.

PSALM LXXXII.

Appeal to Wicked Rulers.

AMID the rulers in the land
The Lord as judge is pleased to stand.
To them he says, "How long will ye
Unjustly judge, and serve the cause
Of men who disobey the laws?
Change ye your course, judge righteously,
Defend the poor and fatherless,
Do justice to those in distress,
The destitute relieve and bless,
And save from th' oppressor's hand;
For they are destitute of light,
And walk in darkness, as of night.
Hence shake th' foundations of the land.
But although gods I might ye call,
Or children of the Lord most high,
Yet ye like other men should die,
And like the helpless princes fall!"
To judge the nations, Lord, arise!
The earth is thine, and at thy mercy lies.

PSALM LXXXIII.

Prayer against Enemies.

KEEP thou not silent, O my God!
  Thy enemies begin to rage;
They confidently spread abroad,
  And in their secret plots engage
Thy people to exterminate,
For them do they intensely hate.
"Let us blot out their name," say they,
  "Till as a nation they may cease,
Nor afterward remembered be!"
The tribes around in league agree,
  No longer satisfied with peace;
The tents of Edom, Ishmael—
  Of Moab, and the Hagarenes,
    With Gebal, Ammon, Amalek,
Philistines, they in Tyre who dwell;
  While with them join Assyrians,
    And would our nation make a wreck!

As th' Midianites let them be,
  Who were each by his fellow slain;
As Jabin's army let them flee,
  Till even one shall not remain;

Or as his captain, Sisera,
Whom Jael in her tent did slay;
　As Oreb and as Zeeb, who,
At Jordan fell to us a prey;
As Zebah and as Zalmunna,
　Whom Gideon, though princes, slew.
For they against us fiercely say,
"Let us God's habitation seize."
Make them as chaff before the wind,
That their assemblies none shall find!
As fire consumes the forest trees,
And makes the lofty mountains blaze,
So let thy tempest them pursue—
Thy storm them greatly terrify!
Till they their faces hide from view,
Ashamed that they such schemes should
　　try;
And turn and seek thy holy name—
Yea, let them soon be put to shame,
Confess that thou art God alone,
Till through the earth thy name is known.

PSALM LXXXIV.

PART I.

Longing for God's Worship.

O THOU our Saviour and our God,
How lovely the place of thine abode!

I long thy sacred courts to see—
My soul cries out, O God, for thee.

The sparrow finds a place of rest,
The swallow where to form her nest;
Yea, in thy house a place she finds,
Beside its altars and its shrines.

Happy are they who spend their days
Here in the service of thy praise;
And thee their strength and glory make,
Nor Zion's holy ways forsake.

The thirsty land through which they go,
They make as a vast fountain flow;
While showers of grace, upon it shed,
It with rich blessings overspread.

And as their journey they pursue,
Their strength they day by day renew;
Till they at last their course fulfill,
And stand secure on Zion's hill.

PART II.

The Value of a Place in God's House.

GOD of thy people, now give ear;
Consent my earnest prayer to hear;
Thou art my shield; O look on me,
Who early was baptized to thee.

Within thy courts a single day,
Exceeds a thousand spent away;
Here better a low place possess,
Than dwell in tents of wickedness.

For in this gloomy moral night,
Thou art a sun to give us light;
And on life's fearful battle-field,
Our ever sure, protecting shield.

Both grace and glory thou wilt give
Us even while on earth we live;
And no good thing to him refuse
Who here the path of right pursues.

O Thou who art most good and just!
The man who puts in thee his trust
Is far above his fellows blessed—
He finds in thee true joy and rest.

PSALM LXXXV.
Prayer for a Revival.

LORD, thou hast in other days
Filled our hearts with joy and praise;
Captives given kind release;
Sin-sick souls afforded peace;

Covered by atoning blood,
Sins that dared thy vengeful sword;
Called those who had gone astray;
Turned from thy fierce wrath away.

Now thy people, Lord, restore;
Angry be with them no more.
Shall thine anger have no end?
Ever shall thy wrath descend?
Us, kept by thy grace alive,
Wilt thou not again revive?
Then thy people shall rejoice—
Praise thee with united voice.

Now thy gracious words we hear,
Bidding us no longer fear,
Nor again to folly turn,
But the words of wisdom learn.
Pleased thou art thine aid to give
Those who in thy service live,
That the glory of our God
Through the earth may spread abroad.

Truth and mercy seek this place,
Righteousness and peace embrace;
Earth shows truth her to commend,
Heaven bids righteousness descend.

God gives us prosperity,
We a rich increase shall see;
He before us leads the way,
We from him need never stray.

PSALM LXXXVI.

PART I.

God's Mercy and Greatness pleaded in Prayer.

O LORD, incline thy gracious ear
   To me in my distress,
For I my life devote to thee;
   Wilt thou not save and bless?

In pity hear my daily cry,
   My troubled soul relieve;
I know, O Lord, that thou art good,
   And ready to forgive:

Yea, that in mercy thou art rich
   To all who call on thee;
Then let my prayer before thee come,
   Let me thy mercy see.

Among the gods there's none like thee;
   No other works like thine;
All nations thou hast made, at last
   Must to thy praise incline.

That thou art great, the One Supreme,
   Thy mighty works declare;
Yea, thou, O Lord, art God alone;
   None can thy glory share.

PART II.

Prayer for Guidance and Protection.

TEACH me thy way, O God, that I
   May walk in truth sincere;
And firmly all my heart unite,
   Thy holy name to fear.

With my whole heart thee will I praise,
   To thee all glory give;
Thy kindness has been great to me—
   It is by thee I live.

Thou hast protected me from death,
   Though in the midst of strife,
When bands of cruel men were formed
   To take away my life.

Thou art a God of graciousness,
   On me compassion have;
Impart thy guarding, conquering strength,
   And me, thy servant, save.

A token of thy favor show,
　　That it my foes may see;
And turn, confounded, when they know
　　That thou, Lord, helpest me.

PSALM LXXXVII.
The Glory of Zion.

ZION, city of my God,
　　On his holy mountain stands,
Looking o'er the earth abroad;
　　Hope and glory of all lands.

Loves he more thy strength and power,
　　Than all else his hands have made;
Thou art as a guarded tower:
　　Glorious things of thee are said!

Life thou dost the nations give;
　　In all lands men spring from thee;
For thy sake alone they live—
　　God has made thee strong and free.

When the world in judgment stands,
　　God will own thy children there;
Joyful come they from all lands—
　　To their home above repair.

PSALM LXXXVIII.

The Prayer of One in Great Distress.

O LORD, thou hast the power to save,
    To me incline thine ear;
By day and night to thee I cry,
    My supplication hear.
My soul is full of misery;
    I draw near to the grave;
Am counted as condemned to death,
    Without a friend to save.
By thy just judgment I am placed
    In an abyss of woe;
Thy weighty wrath upon me rests,
    Thy waves me overflow.
Thou hast my friends from me estranged;
    Escape my power defies;
I languish in my hopelessness,
    And weeping dims mine eyes.

Still to thee, Lord, I lift my hands;
    O do not let me die;
Canst thou thy wonders show the dead?
    Can they to thee draw nigh?
Shall truth be published in the grave?
    Thy goodness there be known?

O Lord, for help to thee I cry;
　I look to thee alone;
At dawn of day on thee I call,
　Thy face why from me hide?
From youth I have afflicted been,
　By dangers terrified.
Yea, now thy wrath me overwhelms,
　Thy terrors fill with awe;
Lover and friend thou hast estranged—
　Acquaintances withdraw.

PSALM LXXXIX.

PART I.

The Subject of the Psalm.

I SING the mercies of the Lord,
　His faithfulness I show;
His mercies evermore endure;
　His truth no change shall know.

He says, "With David I have made
　A covenant secure;
The throne shall in his family
　Remain for ever sure."

PART II.

The Faithfulness and Mercy of God.

THE heavens, O Lord, thy praise show forth,
　The saints thy truth declare;

But who in heaven, or on the earth,
    Can we with God compare?

In the assembled hosts above
    Thou art supremely feared;
And by all creatures on the earth
    Thou shouldst be most revered.

Who mighty is, O God, like thee?
    Or doth his words fulfill?
Thou dost control the raging sea,
    And bid its waves be still.

Thy people, in the days of old,
    Thou didst from bondage free;
But broke in pieces all their foes—
    O'erwhelm'd them in the sea.

The heavens and earth alike are thine;
    Thou didst all things create;
The mountains in thy name rejoice:
    Thou only, Lord, art great.

Justice and equity sustain,
    And make secure thy throne;
Mercy and truth from thee proceed,—
    Are with thee ever known.

PART III.

The People who know the Joyful Sound.

THE Gospel trump to all proclaims,
  God has a ransom found;
And they are more than others blessed
  Who know the joyful sound.

As they their pilgrimage pursue,
  To join the hosts above,
Thou dost, O Lord, their strength renew,
  And look on them in love.

They daily in thy name rejoice,
  For thou hast set them free;
They glory in thy righteousness,
  And put their trust in thee.

Thou art the glory of their strength;
  Strong are they in thy grace;
Yea, through thy favor they stand firm,
  And seek the heavenly place.

Christ for our shield thou hast us given—
  His praise we gladly sing;
He is our richest gift from Heaven,
  Our Saviour and our King.

PART IV.

God's Covenant with David.

A STRONG one I to power have raised,
    And help upon him laid;
Anointed him with holy oil,
    And him a ruler made.

Firmly my hand shall him support,
    Whoever may oppose;
I him will guard from wicked men,
    And beat down all his foes.

My faithfulness shall him exalt,
    My mercy him defend;
And from the rivers to the sea,
    I will his power extend.

He shall me for his Father claim,
    The Rock of his defense;
And I will make him my first-born,
    And power to him dispense.

My mercy toward him shall not fail,
    My words I have made fast;
The throne shall in his house remain
    Long as the heavens last.

And should his children me forsake,
    And violate my law,
I will them punish for their sins,
    But kindness not withdraw.

My covenant I will not break
    Which I with David made;
To him I never will prove false,
    Nor change what I have said.

The throne shall in his family,
    Last as the sun on high;
It is established as the moon,
    The witness in the sky.

PART V.

David Pleads God's Covenant.

BUT now is thine anointed one
    By thee, O Lord, abhorred,
Thou hast his crown cast to the ground,
    Thy covenant made void.

Thou hast his hedges broken down,
    That all may him devour—
Made him to neighbors a reproach,
    And raised his foes to power.

Yea, thou his foes hast made rejoice;
    Thou dost not him defend;

Thou hast brought on him sad defeat,
    His glory to an end.

Thou hast his throne laid in the dust,
    Brought to reproach his name;
Shortened his days of joyous youth,
    And covered him with shame.

How long wilt thou be angry, Lord?
    Against me stand arrayed?
Remember how soon life is passed—
    How frail thou hast us made.

What man that lives shall not see death?
    What man shall shun the grave?
Where is thy loving-kindness now?
    Me from my sorrows save.

Doxology.

Praise ye the great eternal King,
    His sacred name adore;
Join earth and heaven his grace to sing;
    Praise him for evermore.

BOOK IV.

PSALM XC.
The Brevity of Human Life.

O LORD, thou hast our refuge been,
In all the past, from grief and sin.
Before the mountains were brought forth,
Or ever thou hadst formed the earth,
Thou art from all eternity;
And wilt to everlasting be!
Thou takest life from us away,
And biddest all mankind decay.

A thousand ages in thy sight
Are as a brief watch in the night;
As yesterday when it is passed—
With thee years not a moment last:
But man, as with a rapid stream,
Thou bearest hence—he is a dream!
From morn till eve is his short day;
Cut down like grass, and borne away.

For countless sins, all known to thee,
We waste our lives in misery;

Our days thy wrath soon brings to naught,
Our years pass as a rapid thought.
Threescore and ten, allotted here,
Leave only days of pain and fear;
Soon doth remaining strength decay,
Life closes, and we fly away.

Yet who sees in life's brevity
That sin abhorrent is to thee?
Teach us to number so our days,
That we may walk in wisdom's ways.
Turn from thy wrath; O Lord, forgive,
That we may in thy service live;
Grant years of joy for those of pain,
And let our works for thee remain.

PSALM XCI.

The Safety of him who Trusts in God.

HE who trusts the Almighty God,
Has in his shadow safe abode.
Make him thy refuge; in his grace
Thy firm dependence ever place.
He'll guard thee from the fowler's snare,
In pestilence make thee his care;
His sheltering wings above thee spread,
And with his shield protect thy head.

Thou needest fear no plague by night,
No arrow that flies amid the light.
The pestilence may fill the land,
And thousands fall at thy right hand,
But it shall not come nigh to thee;
Only with terror thou shalt see
The recompense Jehovah sends,
On those whose guilt his eye offends.

Since thou hast God thy refuge made,
Thy trust is by his care repaid.
Though others fall, thou shouldst not fear;
No plague shall come thy dwelling near.
His angels he sends from above,
To guard the object of his love;
They round thee form a sacred wall,
And thee uphold lest thou shouldst fall.

"Because he loves me," God doth say,
"I will him guard both night and day;
Deliver from all danger nigh,
And him securely set on high.
When he in trouble calls on me,
To hear him I will present be;
Give honor and long life below,
And him my great salvation show.

PSALM XCII.
A Psalm for the Sabbath-day.

LORD, it is good to come before
Thy throne to worship and adore;
To sing thy praise at early dawn,
And speak thy truth as night comes on;
With instruments to join the voice,
And standing in thy house, rejoice.

Thy goodness is by works expressed,
And them beholding, we are blessed.
Great are thy works displayed around;
Thy purposes, a depth profound;
But erring man, by partial views
Deceived, a fatal course pursues.

For should they who indulge in crime
Here greatly flourish for a time,
It is that they may in the end
To utter wretchedness descend;
And we are led God to adore,
Whose foes thus perish evermore.

The righteous no reverse shall know,
But as the mountain cedars grow;
They, planted in God's house secure,
Are safe, and their support is sure:
The Lord thus shows that he is just,
And blesses all who in him trust.

PSALM XCIII.

God in Nature and in Grace.

THE Lord is clothed with majesty,
    And reigns secure above;
He earth's place fixed by his decree,
    That thence it should not move.

His throne he in the heavens made sure
    Ere time its course began;
And there will ever dwell secure—
    Though Saviour now of man.

The roaring seas their power display;
    The waves majestic roll;
But God is mightier than they,
    And can their rage control.

His word, inspired in every line,
    He potent made to save;
And to its truth, by works divine,
    His testimony gave.

He is well pleased his saints to see,
    And waits while they adore;
Hence they like him should holy be
    Both now and evermore.

PSALM XCIV.

PART I.

Appeal to God against the Wicked.

VENGEANCE belongs to thee;
   O righteous Lord, shine forth!
And recompense iniquity,
   Thou God of all the earth.

How long shall wickedness
   Upon the earth prevail?
Vile lips their insolence express?—
   Shall boasting never fail?

The wicked in their sway,
   Thy heritage oppress;
The widow and the stranger slay,
   And crush the fatherless.

They say, "God doth not see
   Our actions in the land;
Or care for our iniquity,
   And will not us withstand."

PART II.

God's Works Display Himself.

YE who think God sees not,
   Or from concern is free;

That no one can perceive your thought;
    Will ye instructed be?

God's works himself display:
    His skill contrived the ear,
And formed the air sounds to convey—
    Does not this Being hear?

He formed the eye for sight,
    Contrived that it should be
Impressed with images by light—
    Has he not power to see?

Nations his power display;
    He doth their plans inspect,
Opposed to all who disobey—
    And shall not he correct?

He formed the human mind,
    Where thoughts intensely glow,
Or trav'ling thence, leave light behind—
    Shall not this Being know?

God all our words doth hear,
    And all our actions see;
He knows our thoughts; and they appear
    To him as vanity.

PART III.

Chastisement for our Good.

HAPPY, O Lord, is he
   Whom thou correctest here,
To make him wise thy truth to see,
   And thy great name to fear.

His mind is free from care
   In trouble's gloomy day;
Until God shall a pit prepare
   For them who disobey.

God will not them forsake
   Who trust his faithful grace;
His heritage will never make
   A dreary, desert place.

His judgments on the land
   To justice shall return;
To spare his saints God will command,
   His wrath shall cease to burn.

Then the upright in heart,
   Who justice clearly see,
From it shall not through life depart,
   But in it joyful be.

PART IV.

Firm Trust in God.

WHO will rise up with me,
   And wickedness withstand?
Ah! I should ever silent be
   Without God's helping hand.

When it seemed I should fall,
   His goodness held me up;
Afflictions came, but 'mid them all
   He was my constant hope.

He ne'er himself allies
   To men from justice free;
Who mischief in their hearts devise
   Against the powers that be:

Who join the life to take
   Of all the just and good;
Condemn the innocent, and make
   It sport to shed their blood.

The Lord is my strong tower,
   And will me still defend;
The wicked he will hurl from power—
   Bring to a shameful end.

PSALM XCV.

Exhortation to Join in Worship.

COME, let us join in the Saviour's praise,
  He is the firm rock of our trust;
The voice of joy and thanksgiving raise
  To him, the defense of the just.

Creation had by his word its birth;
  He is the great God over all;
In his hands are the depths of the earth;
  The mountains themselves on him call.

The sea he did with its glory crown;
  He molded and formed the dry land;
Let us before our Maker bow down,
  For we are the flock of his hand.

Come ye all people who hear his voice,
  Be not hard and stubborn of heart;
Fix on him your affections and choice,
  And seek in his kingdom a part.

Be ye not like the people perverse,
  Of old who against him transgressed,
Till at last they fell under his curse—
  For ever excluded his rest.

PSALM XCVI.

An Exhortation to Praise God.

TO the Lord sing all the earth,
  And praise his holy name;
His salvation now show forth,
  His glory loud proclaim:
A new song his grace demands;
  O tell his wonders all the day;
Let the people of all lands,
  Bow to his righteous sway.

For the Lord alone is great,
  And greatly to be praised;
All with fear should on him wait,
  To him all hands be raised:
He the heavens above us made;
  Besides him other gods are naught;
To him honor should be paid,
  And to him offerings brought.

Glory and light are his abode;
  The pure before him stand;
O ye saints, proclaim him God;
  And bow at his command:
Give ye him exalted praise,
  And to his courts your off'rings bring;

Worship him, your voices raise,
    And in his presence sing.

Tremble, earth, his throne before;
    Him King, ye nations, own;
Nature, stand, and God adore,
    And make his glory known;
For he doth all things uphold,
    He'll judge the world in righteousness;
Let the heavens he formed of old,
    And earth, their joys express.

Let the seas' vast fullness roar,
    The fields lift up their voice,
Silent be the hills no more,
    Ye forest trees rejoice.
God has come on earth to reign;
    The nations show his faithfulness;
He will justice here maintain,
    And all his people bless.

PSALM XCVII.

Praise to the Supreme Ruler.

REJOICE, O earth! ye isles, be glad!
    Because Jehovah reigns;
Darkness and clouds around him spread,
    Justice his throne sustains:

A burning fire before him goes,
And soon consumes his haughty foes.

His lightnings all the world illume;
　Earth, gazing, greatly fears;
The mountains melt, as wax become,
　When God himself appears:
The heavens his righteousness proclaim,
And nations see, and fear his name.

Idolaters confounded are,
　The gods before him fall;
While Zion hears his voice from far,
　Her daughters him extol:
For he is all the gods above;
His judgments his dread presence prove.

His people should all evil shun,
　And in him ever trust;
For light is for the righteous sown,
　And joy for all the just:
Hence now, ye saints, your God proclaim!
Rejoice, and praise his holy name.

PSALM XCVIII.
A Psalm of Praise.

SING a new song of praise to God,
　Who wond'rous things has done;

For victory he has achieved,
   And made his power known.
His mercy and his truth for us
   Has he recalled to mind;
And all have his salvation seen,
   His good for us designed.

Yea, shout, thou earth, unto the Lord!
   In holy rapture sing!
With harp and voice, in joyful song,
   Praise ye the Lord, our King.
Let mountains, seas, and rivers join,
   And shout and praise again;
For God in truth and righteousness
   Has come on earth to reign.

PSALM XCIX.

Invitation to Engage in Worship.

JESUS reigns, ye nations tremble!
   Sits between the cherubim
Zion's King o'er all exalted;
   Seen by nature's light, though dim:
     He is holy;
   Let all men praise offer him.

He delights in truth and justice,—
   Let his glory all declare;

Equity will he establish;
  Ever for his people care;
    He is holy;
  Bow before his throne in prayer!

Saints of old made supplication,
  And he did an answer send;
He spake from the cloudy pillar,
  Ever ready to defend:
    He is holy;
  On his worship still attend.

They before him made confession,
  And they found his mercy near;
He forgave all their transgression—
  He is ready us to hear;
    He is holy;
  Let us bow in holy fear!

PSALM C.

Grateful Praise and Adoration.

LET all lands their voices raise
In the great Jehovah's praise;
Come his gracious throne before,
Him with reverence adore.

Let all know the Lord is God,
And his name proclaim abroad:

Us he formed when we were naught—
Us, his flock, the Saviour bought.

We who thus to him belong
Joyfully his gates would throng,—
Come to fill his courts with praise,—
Give to him our fleeting days.

Goodness has marked all the past,
Ever shall his mercy last;
And his truth shall stand the same
While endures th' eternal Name.

PSALM CI.

Prayer at Morning Worship.

OF goodness and of justice now,
   O Lord, I fain would sing;
That I may keep the narrow way,
   To thee I still would cling.

Help me to walk within my house
   With uprightness of heart;
To set no wrong before mine eyes,
   Nor from thy truth depart.

All whom I find of ways perverse,
   I will from me remove;
No sland'rer to my bosom take,
   Nor haughty person love.

The pious will I make my friends,
    The upright give employ;
But liars and deceitful ones
    Shall not my peace annoy.

Each morning will I look around,
    Look, too, my heart within,
To see that neither I, nor mine,
    Have fallen into sin.

PSALM CII.

PART I.

Prayer of One in Deep Distress.

O LORD, incline to me thine ear;
    Hide not thy face in my distress;
My life's almost consumed by fear,
    And sorrows deep my heart impress.

Forgetful, I my food forsake;
    My soul in solitude delights;
I doleful lamentations make,
    And sleepless pass the dreary nights.

Me all day long my foes revile;
    Of me as a cursed person speak;
And surely thou hast hid thy smile—
    Left me in ashes thee to seek.

My sins thou dost with wrath repay,
   And me from my high station cast;
My days are passing fast away,
   But thy days evermore will last.

PART II.

Prayer for the Prosperity of Zion.

TO favor Zion, Lord, arise!
   The time has come thou shouldst her bless;
For they who her devotions prize,
   Thy throne in earnest prayer address.

To them a gracious answer send!
   The nations then thy name shall fear;
O build up Zion, her befriend,
   And let thy glory now appear.

The destitute of saving grace
   Now supplication make to thee;
Send from thy high and holy place,
   And let them thy salvation see.

Hear thou the pris'ners' frequent sighs;
   The bound by sin grant kind release;
Then joyful songs to thee shall rise,
   And piety on earth increase.

PART III.

The Immutability of God.

MY days of earthly being wane,
   Borne on by time's resistless flow;
But thou, Lord, dost unchanged remain,
   While generations come and go.

By thee were earth's foundation laid;
   The heavens thy handiwork display;
But all these things which thou hast made
   Are helpless subjects of decay.

Yea, as a garment they wax old;
   None of thy works unchanged abide;
The heavens thou wilt together fold,
   And earth in ruins lay aside.

But thou shalt evermore endure;
   Thou only art unchangeable;
And with thee are thy saints secure,
   As in thy house above they dwell.

PSALM CIII.

A Grateful Song of Praise.

O BLESS the Lord, my soul,
   His holy name adore;

In prayer upon him call;
   Forget his gifts no more:
For they are numberless and free—
   The priceless gifts of grace to thee.

He doth thy sins forgive,
   Thy moral ills remove;
Permits thee here to live,
   And crowns thee with his love:
He ever grants thee heavenly food,
So that each day thy strength's renewed.

Th' oppressed he doth release,
   As in the past made known;
Doth grant abiding peace,
   And as his children own:
Yea, high as are the heavens above,
So great to us has been his love.

Far as from east to west,
   He has our sins removed;
Us pitied when distressed,
   And a kind Father proved:
For well he knows our feeble frame,
Remembers from the dust we came.

Our days are as the grass—
   The spring's first fragile flower,

O'er which the north winds pass,
  And it is known no more:
But ever shall his love endure,
To all his faithful children sure.

Now Him who reigns above,
  Ye mighty angels praise;
Ye saints proclaim his love,
  Rejoicing in his ways;
And all his works loud praise accord:
My soul, too, stand and bless the Lord.

PSALM CIV.

The Wonderful and Manifold Works of God.

MY soul, on God devoutly wait,
And praise his name, for it is great:
Yea, far above all creatures, he
Is clothed with glorious majesty.

The light he as a garment wears;
The heavens spreads out, bedecked with stars;
Above the waters stored on high,
He built the palace of the sky.

The clouds his chariot he makes;
To him the wind's strong wings he takes;

He sends the winds to do his will;
The lightnings his commands fulfill.

The earth's place he arranged secure,
And made its vast foundations sure;
O'er it the mighty waters spread;
But at his stern rebuke they fled.

The valleys sank beneath his hand;
The mountains rose, far spread the land;
Their place he made the waters know,
Lest they again the earth o'erflow.

From springs he sent forth cheerful rills,
And made them run amid the hills,
That beasts which in the forests roam,
To quench their thirst to them might come.

The birds which midst the branches sing,
About them sport on joyous wing;
While ever floating clouds remain,
And satisfy the earth with rain.

Through him its grass earth richly yields,
For all the cattle in the fields;
He causes herbage to spring forth,
And brings, for man, food from the earth.

Man's heart to gladden he gives wine;
And oil to make his face to shine;

And bread nutrition to impart,
And strength and courage give his heart.

The trees so thrifty in the land
Were firmly planted by his hand;
On them the birds their nests prepare,
And wild beasts make their refuge there.

The moon he made the months to show;
The sun its setting hour to know;
When night comes on; and beasts of prey
For food amid the forests stray.

The sun returns, and they withdraw,
Obeying his established law;
And man to labor cheerful goes,
Till eve again brings sweet repose.

Thy works, O Lord, are manifold;
In them thy wisdom we behold;
They all are made with wond'rous skill;
Thy riches all the earth doth fill.

Behold the sea both deep and wide,
Where creatures numberless abide:
Ships learn its strange and trackless ways;
Leviathan within it plays.

On thee for food these hosts depend,
And gather that which thou dost send;
They by thy hand are satisfied,
And perish if thy face thou hide.

Their breath thou takest, and they die;
Thy Spirit sendest from on high,
And into being they spring forth—
Thus thou renewest life on earth.

Thou in thy works rejoicing hast;
Thy glory evermore shall last;
Earth shakes when thou dost on it look;
The hills thou touchest, and they smoke.

Long as I live to God I'll sing—
Accept Thou now my offering;
Be wickedness on earth destroyed;
Rejoice, my soul; O praise the Lord!

PSALM CV.

The Goodness of God to Israel traced in their History.

GIVE thanks to God, upon him call,
 He is our rightful King;
His works to all the world make known,
 And to him joyful sing.

Yea, glory in his holy name,
    And triumph in his grace;
O let your hearts in him rejoice,
    And seek ye now his face.
Remember all the wond'rous works
    Which he for us has done,
His chosen people on the earth;
    For great is every one.
Jehovah is himself our God;
    His judgments far extend;
His covenant he'll bear in mind
    Till generations end.
It first with Abraham he made,
    With Isaac then renewed,
And then to Jacob reaffirmed
    That he would make it good.
He said, "To thee and to thy seed
    I Canaan truly give;
That ye, despite your many foes,
    May there in plenty live."

And when in number they were few,
    And strangers in the land,
Them, as they passed from place to place,
    He guarded with his hand.
Kings for their sake did he rebuke,
    That none should them oppress;

Saying, "Do not my people harm—
　My prophets not distress."

When he brought famine on the land,
　And broke the staff of bread;
He, sending one before them forth,
　Provision for them made.
Joseph was for a bondsman sold,
　His feet with chains were bound,
Till his predictions came to pass,
　And he was truthful found.
Then to his prison sent the king,
　And him from chains set free;
And made him ruler in the land,
　Next to his majesty;
That all the interests of his realm,
　He wisely should conduct;
To bind his princes as he would,
　And counselors instruct.

Then Israel to Egypt came,
　To sojourn in the land;
And there God greatly them increased,
　And mighty made their hand:
But the Egyptians changed from friends
　To be their bitter foes;
And in their hatred brought on them
　Insufferable woes.

Moses and Aaron then were sent,
  Them from the land to bring;
And many mighty works they wrought
  Before the haughty king.
The Lord sent darkness on the land,
  Their evil hearts to try;
He turned their water into blood,
  And caused their fish to die.
He sent forth frogs, a mighty host,
  Which them deprived of rest;
He spake, and there came flies and lice,
  Their dwellings to infest.
Instead of rain he sent them hail;
  He fire upon them sent;
And in his anger smote their vines,
  And all their fig-trees rent.
Obedient to his command,
  Locusts upon them poured;
Which spread themselves throughout the land,
  And all their fruits devoured.
Then he their first-born smote with death,
  And Israel set free;
Before ordaining in their tribes
  That none should feeble be.
With gold and silver they went forth,
  While God was still their guide;

And Egypt gladly let them go,
    For they were terrified.

God spread a cloud o'er them by day,
    A fire for light by night:
Gave flocks of quails to satisfy
    Their craving appetite.
The rock he opened, and brought forth
    Water their thirst to slake;
For he, remembering the past,
    His promise would not break.
He led his people forth with joy,
    The Gentiles dispossessed;
The lands of others gave their tribes,
    With others' labors blessed;
That they might still his name preserve,
    And his just laws obey:
Hence for past mercies offer praise;
    For present favors pray.

PSALM CVI.

A Historic Sketch of the Sins of Israel.

PRAISE ye the Lord, for he is good,
    His mercy never ends;
Who can his mighty deeds declare?
    The blessings which he sends?

Who fully can show forth his praise?
　　Him worthily address?—
They happy are who justice do,
　　And practice righteousness.
With favors promised to thy saints,
　　O Lord, remember me;
And with thy great salvation bless;
　　Yea, grant that I may see
Thy chosen people free again,
　　And prosperous in the land;
That I may in their joy rejoice,
　　And safely with them stand.

We have with all our fathers sinned
　　Who were from Egypt brought;
Thy wonders did they disregard,
　　Thy mercies they forgot;
Rebelled against thee at the sea,
　　In dangers threat'ning hour;
Yet saved he them for his name's sake,
　　And to make known his power.
For them he then dried up the sea,
　　And led them safely through;
But in the waters, flowing back,
　　Their enemies o'erthrew.
Then they believed his promises,
　　And joyful sang his praise;

But soon his mercies they forgot,
   And walked in sinful ways.
They did to appetite give way,
   For meat distrustful beg;
And he them granted their request,
   But sent, meantime, a plague.

Against their leaders they rebelled,
   And were by earth devoured;
A fire was kindled in their midst—
   God's wrath was on them poured.
They made an image of a calf,
   And to it worship paid;
Thus they, like to a grazing ox,
   The Lord of glory made!
Their mighty Saviour they forgot,
   Who wond'rous things had done,
From their Egyptian bondage freed,
   And victory for them won;
When them God threatened to destroy;
   But Moses for them prayed,
And stood before him in the breach,
   Till he his wrath allayed.
They, too, the promised land despised,
   And disbelieved his word;
With murmuring turned from his voice,
   As though they had not heard.

Then he swore they should never come
    Into the promised rest;
And their descendants scattered be,
    And in all lands oppressed.
They Baal-peor worshiped, too;
    His sacrifices ate;
When God them to the plague gave up,
    And fearful made their fate.
But Phinehas avenged their crime,
    So that the plague was stayed;
For which he was imputed just,
    And honors were him paid.
They also sinned at Meribah,
    And ill on Moses brought;
For he spake there imprudently—
    Without sufficient thought.

They spared the nations when they came
    Into the promised land,
And learned their evil practices;
    Thus breaking God's command.
They even to their idols bowed
    And offered sacrifice
Of their own children, by them slain—
    A most revolting vice!
Polluting thus the land with blood,
    The blood of innocence;

For idols, too, forsaking God,
  Till his wrath waxed intense.
And with abhorrence them he gave
  Up to their foes a prey;
To be oppressed and sadly crushed
  Beneath their cruel sway.
And oft did he deliver them;
  But they his laws transgressed;
And then he gave them up again
  To be again oppressed.
Yet when they in affliction cried,
  He heard their earnest prayer;
His covenant remembered then,
  And made them still his care.
According to his mercy great,
  Again he set them free;
And caused their foes to pity them
  In their captivity.

Lord, from the nations gather us,
  And holy make our ways;
Then we will offer thanks to thee,
  And glory in thy praise.

BOOK V.

PSALM CVII.
God's Goodness to Men in Different Circumstances.

UNTO the Lord thank-off'rings give,
  He only is supremely good;
His mercy evermore shall live:
  And let it be proclaimed abroad
  By all who are redeemed of God
From the strong foe's oppressive hand;
Gathered again from every land,
Where exiled they had been oppressed;
From north, and south, and east, and west.

They wandered in a desert land,
  Where reigned unbroken solitude;
  And where they found not proper food
  When hungry and athirst, nor road,
Nor guidance of a friendly hand,
  To a safe city where to dwell.
Then they besought God them to save,
And he deliv'rance kindly gave.
  He guided them o'er hill and dell,
  And still provided for them well.

O let them God's great goodness praise,
And glory in his wondrous ways,
For he the thirsty satisfies,
And them who hunger ne'er denies.

They dwelt in darkness most profound
    Of dungeons, where they were confined,
And in chains and afflictions bound,
    Because against the Lord they sinned.
(For they defied his righteous will,
And did not his commands fulfill;)
Until their hearts were filled with grief—
They fell, and none brought them relief.
Then they besought God them to save,
And he deliv'rance kindly gave.
From their dark cells he did them take,
And their strong bands asunder brake.
O let them God's great goodness praise,
And glory in his wondrous ways,
For he has set the pris'ner free;
Released from chains and misery.

The foolish God's just laws transgressed,
And hence were punished and distressed;
When they turned languidly from good,
And even loathed the best of food;
And panting, labored for their breath
While lying near the gates of death.

Then they besought God them to save,
And he deliv'rance kindly gave.
He came to them, rebuked their pain,
And them restored to health again.
O let them God's great goodness praise,
And glory in his wondrous ways;
Let thanks their tuneful lips employ,
And all his works declare with joy.

They who afar in vessels sail,
   And business do upon the sea,
Behold God's works amid the gale—
   His terror and his majesty.
He sends his strong command abroad;
The winds obey the word of God,
And lift the mighty waves on high.
Then mount they up as to the sky,
   Then sink into the deep again,
   Till hope refuses to remain;
They stagger like a drunken man,
And find they no relief can plan,
   For all their wonted skill is vain.
Then they beseech God them to save,
And he bestows the good they crave.
He calms the storm, and o'er the sea
Far round them spreads tranquillity—

Them gladdens till each joyful sings,
And to their destined haven brings.
O let them God's great goodness praise,
And glory in his wondrous ways!
Before the saints, O let them sing
The praises of their God and King.

He rivers turns into dry ground,
And springs in deserts bids abound.
A fruitful land he barren makes,
　For sins which were committed there;
But never he the just forsakes,
　But for them doth a place prepare,
Where they may fields and vineyards own,
　Which yield a plentiful increase;
There makes to them his goodness known,
　And grants to the obedient peace.
And when they are for sins brought low,
　He doth contempt on princes pour,
And makes them through wild deserts go,
　But raises up the pious poor,
And makes their families increase,
And all their sad afflictions cease.
This with great joy the righteous see;
While silenced is iniquity.
Whoso is wise, let him observe,
And God on earth devoutly serve.

PSALM CVIII.
Exultation in God's Goodness.

NOW strengthened is my heart, O Lord!
 I'll make thy mercies known;
Awake, my soul! my harp, awake!
 I will awake at dawn.
Among the nations thee I'll praise,
 Among the kingdoms sing;
Thy mercy reaches to the heavens,
 Thy truth the clouds, O King!
And now in thee I put my trust,
 Protect me in thy ways;
Thy name above the heavens exalt,
 Above the earth thy praise.
Thy promises rejoice my heart,
 On them my hope I stay;
The tribes around shall to me yield,
 And own my rightful sway.
Who will me lead against my foes?
 Bring to the city strong?
Wilt thou not, who didst us forsake,
 For deeds unjust and wrong?
O aid thou us in our distress!
 For help of man is vain;
Through thee we shall do valiantly,
 And soon the victory gain.

PSALM CIX.

Invective against Enemies.

BE thou not silent, O my God!
   For wicked men against me rise,
   And such as take delight in lies;
Yea, they who hate me spread abroad,
And me assault on every side,
   Though I have given them no cause.
   My virtues move not their applause;
They for my kindness me deride;
   They curse me while for them I pray;
   My love with bitter hate repay.

O God, mine adversary see;
   For counselor at his right hand
   Let his dire foe in favor stand,
And over him the wicked be.
Let condemnation on him fall;
   His very prayer account a crime;
   And may he die before his time;
And beggars be his children all!
Let creditors his substance seize,
   And none to mercy be inclined;
   No pity may his children find;
And let not aught thy wrath appease,

Until thou dost his name erase,
And make unknown his dwelling-place.
   His ancestry's misdeeds repay,
   And let their memory decay;
Because he did no pity show,
Nor for the poor compassion know;
   The broken-hearted sought to slay,
And cursing loved. O let it fall
On him, and round him like a pall
   Extend, and his dread clothing be:
Let it engirdle him around.
Yea, may such recompense be found,
   By all who evil speak of me!

   Thus, O my God, take thou my part!
In trouble do not me forsake,
But guard me for thy own name's sake;
   For great in mercy, Lord, thou art.
Now I am brought exceeding low,
Languid in poverty and woe;
   Within me bleeds my wounded heart.
I am ejected like a pest;
As a declining shadow waste;
My flesh is quite consumed away,
While frequently I fast and pray.
My enemies do me revile,
And gazing, shake their heads the while.

O God, give them to understand
That in this is thy mighty hand;
And while they curse, O do thou bless;
Deliver me from my distress.
When they rise up, put them to shame;
Let ignominy blast their name,
And o'er them like a mantle spread,
Till they are wholly loathsome made!
Then I will gladly thee confess,
And in the congregation bless;
For thou dost still the poor defend—
Of justice the eternal friend.

PSALM CX.

Regal and Sacerdotal Powers of Christ.

UNTO my Lord Jehovah spake,
 "Sit thou at my right hand,
Till I thy foes thy footstool make!"
 And he will through the land,
From Zion far extend thy sway,
Till all thy foes shall thee obey.

And ready shall thy people be,
 Thy kingly power to own,
When they thy mighty forces see,
 And thy dread power is known:

Thy young men shall like dew spring forth,
Which morning spreads o'er all the earth.

And to my Lord Jehovah swore,
    And he will not repent;
"Thou art a priest for evermore!"
    Thy power has this extent;
Not only o'er mankind to reign,
But them bring back to God again.

Jehovah is at thy right hand;
    Thou shalt thy foes subdue,
Spread righteousness throughout the land,
    And form the world anew:
For thy resourses are divine,
And power omnipotent is thine.

PSALM CXI.

A Sacramental Hymn.

WITH God's people joyful sing,
Praise our Saviour and our King;
Great the works which he has done,
Glorious is every one.
But his other wondrous deeds
Man's redemption far exceeds;
Studied by the hosts above,
Us subduing with his love.

Just and gracious, Lord, thou art,
Mercy ready to impart;
Righteousness is now secure,
And shall evermore endure;
While compassion offers grace
To our fallen, sinful race :
Love and justice thus combine;
Meet in harmony divine.

A memorial is given
Of this gracious work of Heaven;
An enduring, sacred rite,
Us to strengthen and delight.
All who come with heart sincere,
Are of God fed amply here;
He is merciful and kind,
Bears his covenant in mind.

He his saints has favor showed
By the power on them bestowed;
He'll to them the world subdue,
And in righteousness renew.
Truth and justice ever stand,
Safely guarded by his hand;
Long shall his commands endure,
And his covenant is sure.

Yea, redemption's works shall last,
When the things of time are past;

For he ever is the same,
Holy and revered his name.
Wisdom in his fear begins,
Who atoned for all our sins;
Hence now sing his worthy praise—
It shall last through endless days.

PSALM CXII.

Prosperity of the Righteous.

PRAISE ye the Lord! for he doth bless
Him who delights in righteousness;
Prosperity shall him attend,
And to his children long descend.

In darkness light to him shall rise,
For he doth liberal things devise;
Compassion reigns within his breast,
And sympathy for the distressed.

When he in judgment is arraigned,
His cause is fully then sustained;
He ever will remembered be,
Receiving favors rich and free.

He need not evil tidings fear,
For God, protecting him, is near;
He freely to the needy gives,
And in great peace and honor lives.

The wicked with vexation see
His undisturbed prosperity;
Until they at the last expire,
Deprived through life of their desire.

PSALM CXIII.

Praise ye the Lord.

PRAISE ye the Lord, all ye his saints!
　Praise him for evermore!
From the rising to the setting sun
　His holy name adore.

The nations all his subjects are;
　He reigns above the sky;
Who is like to the Lord our God
　In his abode on high?

With condescension he stoops down,
　While splendors round him glow,
To see what passes in the heavens,
　And on the earth below.

The poor he raises from the dust
　By his controlling hand;
And gives an honored place among
　The princes of the land.

The house he blesses of the just,
　And grants a rich reward:
Of all his mercies joyful sing!
　Again praise ye the Lord!

PSALM CXIV.

Israel coming out of Egypt.

WHEN God did Israel redeem,
　And out of Egypt take,
Where they had with a people dwelt,
　Who a strange language spake,
His sanctuary Jacob was,
　And Israel his realm:
The sea beheld, and frightened fled;
　It would not them o'erwhelm.
And Jordan, too, turned swiftly back—
　Would not obstruct their way;
The mountains leaped out of their place,
　The hills like lambs at play.

What ailed thee, O thou mighty sea,
　That still thou didst not lay?
And Jordan, that thou turnedst back
　When in the people's way?
And mountains, that ye leaped about,
　And hills, like lambs at play?

Tremble, O earth, before the Lord!
  Ye nations, be afraid!
He turned the rock into a lake,
  The flint a fountain made.

PSALM CXV.

The Lord in Contrast with Idols.

NOT unto man, but unto God,
  Ye people, honor pay;
For his great mercy and truth's sake,
  Why should the nations say,
    Where is their God?

Our God is in the heavens above,
  And all the world commands;
Their idols gold and silver are,
  The work of human hands:
    They are not God.

Their eyes see not, nor hear their ears,
  Nor mouths have power to talk;
They noses, hands, and feet possess:
  But smell, handle, and walk,
    They cannot do.

They who make them, and in them trust,
  Are like them, false and vain;

O Israel, trust in the Lord!
   He will our rights maintain:
      He is our shield.

O house of Aaron, trust the Lord!
   And ye who fear his name!
He will be mindful of us still,
   And guard from woe and shame:
      On him rely.

The house of Israel he'll help,
   The house of Aaron bless;
And all who fear his holy name
   Shall good on earth possess;
      Both small and great.

You and your children he'll increase,
   And bless you more and more:
The Lord for his great mercies praise;
   Supremely him adore
      Who all things made!

The highest heaven is the Lord's,
   The earth to man he gave;
The dead cannot praise offer him;
   They who lie in the grave
      Silent remain.

But we, the people of his choice,
   And favored ones on earth,
Will serve the Lord, and bless his name,
   Even from this time forth:
     Praise ye the Lord!

PSALM CXVI.

PART I.

On Trusting God when in Distress.

1 IN the Lord my God rejoice,
   Who doth my prayer receive;
And will call on his holy name
   While on the earth I live.

The snares of death encompassed me,
   And pains tormenting seized;
Then on the Lord in prayer I called,
   And he to hear was pleased.

The Lord is merciful and kind,
   Ready his saints to bless;
He me preserved in danger's hour,
   And helped me in distress.

Return unto thy rest, my soul!
   The voice of prayer he hears;
He me preserved from threatened death,
   And kept mine eye from tears.

He made me in his grace stand firm,
   And in his truth remain;
For in my deep distress I said,
   "All human trust is vain."

PART II.

Hymn for Social Worship.

WHAT shall I render to the Lord
   For all his gifts to me?
I will the cup of salvation take,
   And call, O God, on thee.

Yea, now the vows which I have made
   I to the Lord will pay;
And in the presence of his saints
   Will sing, and speak, and pray.

In all his pious worshipers,
   God ever takes delight;
He watches o'er them, and their life
   Is precious in his sight.

Hear now my earnest prayer, O Lord!
   For I belong to thee;
Thou hast loosed all the bonds of sin,
   And kindly set me free.

Hence thee I will devoutly praise,
  Who dost such grace afford;
Yea, in thy courts I'll raise my voice—
  Praise ye, O praise, the Lord!

PSALM CXVII.

A Psalm of Praise.

YE nations, praise the Lord,
  His holy name confess;
Ye people, all with one accord
  Your God devoutly bless!

For he toward us is kind,
  While truth gives to his word
Th' unchanging impress of his mind—
  Praise ye, O praise the Lord!

PSALM CXVIII.

PART I.

Confidence in the Divine Protection.

GIVE thanks to God, for he is good,
  His promises are sure;
"For ever," let all people say,
  "His goodness shall endure."

I called upon him in distress,
　　And he deliv'rance gave;
Yea, he is my abiding friend,
　　And me delights to save.

He is the helper of his saints,
　　And doth for them provide;
Better it is in him to trust,
　　Than in mere man confide.

The nations all against me rise,
　　Like bees encompass me;
Them in God's name will I destroy!
　　They shall his terrors see!

PART II.

Praise after Victory.

MY foes assailed me, but were slain;
　　God did me favor show;
He is my glory and my song—
　　I him salvation owe.

Hence in the temples of his saints
　　These words of praise shall be:
"Exalted is the Lord's right hand!
　　It doeth valiantly!"

And now I know I shall not die,
   But live God's works to show;
For though he sorely chastened me,
   He stayed death's fatal blow.

Open the gates of righteousness,
   That I may enter in;
Then fervent praise will I address
   To Him who saves from sin.

PART III.

Christ the Corner-Stone.

HE now is made the corner-stone
   The builders did despise:
This is the mighty work of God,
   And wondrous in our eyes.

And this is God's appointed day;
   O let us joyful be;
And with united voices pray,
   "Lord, send prosperity."

Blessed be our Rock, the mighty One,
   Who from God's presence came!
Him in his house let us adore,
   And bless his sacred name.

Jehovah light has on us shed;
  Bind ye the sacrifice,
That the atonement may be made—
  Be paid redemption's price.

Praise now I offer, Lord, to thee;
  Thou righteous art and pure;
And changeless to eternity,
  Thy goodness shall endure.

PSALM CXIX.

PART I.

The Righteous greatly Blessed.

HAPPY are they whose ways are pure,
  Nor from God's laws depart;
Who all his ordinances keep
  In singleness of heart.

With care they shun iniquity,
  Obeying his command;
And ever speak and do as they
  His precepts understand.

O Lord, thou art my guide! to keep
  Thy statutes me direct;
For only can I shame avoid
  When I thy laws respect.

But with full heart I can thee praise,
    Whose law my guide I make;
Help me to keep thy statutes then,
    And never me forsake.

PART II.

Means of Moral Purity.

HOW shall a young man keep his way
    Pure from polluting stain?
By taking proper heed to it,
    As in thy word made plain.

With my whole heart I sought thee, Lord;
    May I not go astray;
But thy word treasure in my heart,
    Lest thee I disobey.

Bless'd be thy great and holy name!
    Thou wilt me knowledge give;
So shall my lips the truths proclaim
    I from thy mouth receive.

Thine ordinances greater joy
    Than riches do afford;
Hence in them seek I my delight,
    And treasure up thy word.

PART III.

The Courage of the Righteous.

DEAL kindly with thy servant, Lord;
  In thy law make me wise:
That I deep things in it may see,
  O open thou mine eyes!

I am a pilgrim on the earth;
  Hide not thy truths from me;
For I had fainted, but for hope
  That I thy law should see.

Thou dost rebuke the vainly proud
  Who from thy precepts stray;
But that I may their shame avoid,
  Me in thy statutes stay.

Though princes should against it speak,
  I will thy law receive:
Thine ordinances me delight,
  And counsel to me give.

PART IV.

Prayer for Divine Aid.

MY soul is bow'd down to the dust;
  According to thy word,

Revive thou me! Thy truth I've taught,
   And thou, O Lord, hast heard.

Help me to see the righteous way;
   Thy works should give me hope:
As thou hast promised in thy word,
   From trouble lift me up.

From error's way my feet remove;
   Thy law to me make known;
For I prefer the way of truth:
   Be it my guide alone.

I to thine ordinances cleave;
   Protect from shameful charge:
Secure in duty's path I'll run
   If thou my heart enlarge.

PART V.

Piety Better than Wealth.

TEACH me, O Lord, the way of truth,
   Lest from it I depart;
Give me to understand thy law,
   And keep it near my heart.

In thy commandments lead me forth,
   My joy may they remain;

And to thy ways incline my heart,
  More than to love of gain.

From vanity turn thou mine eyes,
  Me quicken in thy way;
Fulfill thy faithful promises,
  For I do thee obey.

Turn the reproach I fear away;
  Thy statutes all are right;
With eagerness I long for them;
  May they my soul delight.

PART VI.

The Safety of Obedience.

O LORD, thy mercies grant to me
  According to thy word,
That I may answer give with ease
  To censures I have heard.

Remove not from my mouth thy word,
  For in it is my trust;
So shall I keep, without offense,
  Thy law, forever just.

Thou wilt make safe and sure my path,
  For I thy precepts seek;

Then I to nobles shall not fear
    Thy precious word to speak.

Now thy commandments, which I love,
    With joy my soul elate;
I all thy precepts long to know,
    And in them meditate.

PART VII.

Delight in God's Law.

REMEMBER, Lord, thy promises,
    For they are now my hope;
They in affliction comfort give,
    And lift my spirit up.

The proud me in derision have,
    Yet to thy law I cling;
I think of all thy judgments past,
    And of thy mercies sing.

Within me indignation burns,
    When vice my thoughts engage;
Thy statutes are my joyful song
    Through all my pilgrimage.

At night, while thinking of thy name,
    More dear to me than sleep,
It doth afford me comfort great,
    That I thy precepts keep.

PART VIII.

Constancy of the Righteous.

THOU art my portion, O my God;
 I in thy law am staid;
And I in prayer the promise plead
 Which thou to me hast made.

I meditate on all thy ways,
 Turn to thy laws my feet,
And haste thy just commands to keep,
 Thy righteous claims to meet.

Though snares the wicked round me spread,
 I cling still to thy cause;
Yea, rise at midnight thee to praise
 For all thy righteous laws.

They my companions are who fear
 The Lord to disobey:
The earth is of thy goodness full;
 Teach me thy righteous way.

PART IX.

The Use of Afflictions.

O LORD, thou dost thy servant bless,
 As thou hast promise made;

Sound knowledge teach me, for my faith
  Upon thy word is stayed.

Before affliction on me came,
  Oft-times I went astray;
But good are all thy dealings, Lord;
  Hence I would thee obey.

Though lies the proud against me forge,
  I turn not from the right;
Their heart is wholly void of sense;
  I, in thy law delight!

Afflictions are in mercy sent;
  They thy just ways unfold;
And better is thy law to me
  Than richest stores of gold.

PART X.

God's Judgments Just.

I AM the creature of thy hands;
  Teach me thy precepts just,
That they who see me may rejoice;
  For in thy word I trust.

I know thy judgments all are right;
  Thou dost afflict for good;
Thy loving-kindness grant me now,
  According to thy word.

Thy mercies cause me now to live;
  Thy law is my delight:
Confound and put to shame the proud,
  But guide my thoughts aright.

Let them who fear thee come to me,
  That they thy laws may learn;
My heart make perfect in thy word,
  Lest shame my cheek should burn.

PART XI.

Trust in God's Providence.

MY soul for thy salvation longs;
  O Lord, I trust in thee;
I ever to thy promise look,
  Wilt thou not comfort me?

Though loathsome by affliction made,
  I'm not from thee estranged;
And may I not, by thy dread power,
  Be of my foes avenged?

They who do not regard thy law
  Lay schemes me to ensnare;
But true and faithful is thy word—
  On thee I cast my care.

And though they me almost destroyed,
   Yet me this did not move;
O strengthen me to keep thy law,
   According to thy love.

PART XII.

Perfection of God's Law.

FOREVER, Lord, thy word abides,
   Fixed as the heavens secure;
Thy faithfulness from age to age
   Shall as the earth endure.

Thy mighty works secure remain,
   They subject are to thee;
But I had perished, had thy law
   Not been support to me.

I ne'er thy precepts will forget,
   For they my soul revive;
O help me now, for I am thine;
   To me thy precepts give.

For me the wicked lie in wait;
   Still is my trust in God;
Though no perfection earth affords,
   Thy law's exceeding broad!

PART XIII.
God's Law makes Wise.

THY holy law, O Lord, I love,
    And study all the day;
It raises me my foes above—
    I wiser am than they.

Having thine ordinances learned,
    My teachers I excel;
Less wise the ancients were than I,
    Nor knew thy law as well.

That I might rightly keep thy word,
    I have from evil fled;
Yea, I depart not from thy law,
    But by it still am led.

I love thy gracious words, O Lord;
    Sweet to my taste are they;
I from thy precepts wisdom learn,
    Lest I should go astray.

PART XIV.
A Light to our Path.

A LAMP thy word is to my feet,
    And to my path a light;
And I my fervent vows will keep,
    It to observe aright.

Yet sad afflictions on me press—
  O Lord, my soul revive!
Accept the offerings of my mouth,
  And me instruction give.

My life is ever in my hand,
  Dread snares beset my way;
Yet will I not forget thy law,
  Nor from thy precepts stray.

Thy ordinances are my wealth,
  And comfort of my heart;
And while my earthly being lasts
  I'll not from thee depart.

PART XV.

Pious Regard for God's Law.

I HATE vain thoughts and impious men,
  While thy just law I love;
Thou art my shield and hiding-place;
  I shall thy goodness prove.

Ye evil-doers, get ye hence!
  I will God's law obey;
But lest my hope make me ashamed,
  Uphold me in thy way.

If thy just statutes I respect,
  I shall secure remain;

But they shall perish who turn back,
  For their deceit is vain.

To thee the wicked are as dross,
  Hence I thy laws revere;
I in thy presence stand with awe,
  And thy dread judgments fear.

PART XVI.

Waiting for God's Blessing.

TO mine oppressors yield me not,
  For I thy laws respect;
Let not the proud o'er me prevail,
  But from my foes protect.

Mine eyes fail while to thee I look,
  And for thy promise wait;
Thy statutes teach me, Lord; nor yield
  Me to a cruel fate.

I would thy statutes understand;
  Me toward them ever draw;
It now is time for thee to act,
  For men make void thy law.

But I thy just commandments love
  More than the finest gold.
In all things I regard them right,
  Nor vice would I behold.

PART XVII.

God's Law a Vast Deep.

THY laws amazing depths display,
    Hence I observe them still;
The entrance of thy word gives light,
    It teaches us thy will.

For thy commandments, Lord, I pant;
    Thy promises I claim;
For thou hast ever gracious been
    To them who love thy name.

To thee my footsteps kindly draw,
    That I secure may stand;
From all oppression set me free,
    And in thy ways command.

Me, by thy cheering light divine,
    Wise in thy statutes make;
For I am grieved that sinful men
    Cease not thy law to break.

PART XVIII.

God's Law Just and True.

O LORD, thou righteous art and true,
    And just are all thy laws;
Thine ordinances all are good—
    Thine is a holy cause.

Because my foes forget thy law,
    I am consumed of zeal;
For thy word, holy, just, and good,
    Intensest love I feel.

I am of low and mean estate,
    And thee regard with awe;
For perfect righteousness is thine,
    And true thy sacred law.

While fearful troubles me assail,
    Thy law is my delight;
In it me understanding give,
    For safety is in right.

PART XIX.

Longing for God's Law.

MY prayers for strength to know thy law,
    O Lord, be pleased to hear;
To thee I for salvation cry,
    Incline to me thine ear.

Oft ere the morning dawns, in prayer
    I for thy promise wait;
Yea, the night-watches, for calm thought,
    Mine eyes anticipate.

In loving-kindness me renew,
    And to my prayer attend;
Lo, they who hate me now are near—
    Me from the proud defend.

Thou nearer art than they, O Lord;
    Thy promises are sure;
The ordinances of thy house
    Shall evermore endure.

PART XX.

Grief for Others' Disobedience.

I DO not, Lord, thy law forget
    In sad affliction's hour;
As thou hast promised, me revive,
    And save me by thy power.

The wicked shall no safety find,
    For they thy statutes break;
But kindly thou wilt me revive,
    For thine own justice' sake.

Many and cruel are my foes,
    Yet I thy laws obey;
And I am filled with wasting grief
    When others go astray.

O yes, I love thy precepts, Lord;
  Let grace my strength renew;
Thy statutes ever shall endure,
  For they are just and true.

PART XXI.

God Praised for his Law.

PRINCES oppose, yet I thy word
  Regard with awe profound;
In it my heart rejoices, too,
  As one great spoils has found.

Lying I hate, but love the law
  To man revealed from heaven;
And seven times a day I'll praise
  Thee for thy statutes given.

Great peace have they who love thy law,
  They shall securely stand;
And hence I wait on thee, and do
  As thou dost me command.

Thine ordinances I observe;
  They all to me are dear;
Thy holy precepts I obey,
  And walk with thee sincere.

PART XXII.
God's Law our Happiness.

NOW let my prayer before thee come,
  Thy promised blessing give;
I supplication make to thee,
  Let me thy grace receive.

When thou dost teach thy law to me,
  My lips pour forth thy praise;
My tongue, too, of thy word shall sing,
  While I walk in thy ways.

Now let thy hand afford me help;
  Thy law my choice is made;
And it shall ever me delight:
  Grant me thy saving aid.

O let me live thy name to praise!
  Thy judgments me sustain;
Sought when astray, I thee will love,
  Nor break thy laws again.

PSALM CXX.
Complaints concerning Enemies.

DISTRESS'D, O Lord, on thee I call;
  Do thou an answer send;

And now from falsehood and deceit
 Me graciously defend.

What profit, wicked man, on thee
 Will thy false tongue confer,
Though like sharp arrows of the strong,
 And coals of juniper?

Alas for me, that I sojourn
 Amid deceitful foes!
While I would be on friendly terms,
 They fiercely peace oppose.

PSALM CXXI.

Confidence in Divine Protection.

UP to the hills where God resides,
 By whom all things were made,
I lift mine eyes in fervent prayer,
 And seek his saving aid.

Lest I should fall, or from him stray,
 Me he will safely keep;
For the Protector of his saints
 Needs neither rest or sleep.

He is their shade at their right hand,
 And doth in them delight;
The sun shall not them smite by day,
 Neither the moon by night.

In all the various ills of life,
   Them still his care is o'er;
Their going out and coming in
   He watches evermore.

PSALM CXXII.
Pray for the Peace of Zion.

I WAS glad to hear them say,
   Let us to God's house repair;
Here I would for ever stay,
   And engage in praise and prayer.

Built by the Almighty's hand,
   Zion stands secure and strong;
And the saints in every land
   To it come with joyful song.

Here is heard th' unyielding law,
   And the words of Gospel grace;
While the judgment throne with awe
   Fills this solemn, sacred place.

For the peace of Zion pray!
   May they prosper who love thee!
Let the saints united say,
   "With thee be prosperity!"

Now I for my brethren's sake
  Say, "Within thee be there peace!
Thee may God still stronger make—
  Ever let thy joys increase!"

PSALM CXXIII.
Prayer for Divine Mercy.

WE look to him who dwells on high;
  No other help have we;
As servants to their masters look,
  So, Lord, we look to thee.

And thus we ever will look up
  Till thou thy blessing send;
In pity now look down on us,
  And to our prayers attend.

On us have mercy, O our God,
  For sorrow us o'erflows;
We sink beneath the insolence
  Of our reproachful foes.

PSALM CXXIV.
Exultation in God's Goodness.

HAD God not been with us,
  Now may his people say,
We to our cruel enemies
  Had been an easy prey.

Round us the waters rose,
    And over us had passed
Had not our God their rage withstood,
    And firmly held them fast.

Blessed be the Lord who did
    For us thus interpose;
So that, as from the fowler's snare,
    We have escaped our foes.

The snare was broken soon,
    For God gave us his aid—
Jehovah is our faithful friend,
    By whom all things were made.

PSALM CXXV.

Their Safety who Trust in God.

THEY who trust in the Lord
    Shall like Mount Zion be;
Which naught can move, but stands secure
    As God's eternity.

As round Jerusalem
    The mountains firmly stand,
So ever God surrounds his saints,
    And guards them with his hand.

On us he'll not allow
   The wicked to aggress;
Lest any of his yielding saints
   Should learn their wickedness.

O Lord, to them do good
   Who upright are in heart!
Among us let all wavering cease,
   And grace to all impart.

PSALM CXXVI.

The Captive's Return.

WHEN God brought back his captives,
   We were like them that dream;
Our mouths he filled with laughter,
   Salvation was our theme.

And then said all the nations,
   "God doth them greatly bless!"
Yea, God has blessed us greatly,
   We joyfully confess.

O bring back all our captives,
   Like streams in a dry land!
May they who sowed in sorrow
   Reap with a joyful hand.

Sure, he who goes forth weeping,
  With precious seed to sow,
Shall come again rejoicing,
  With many sheaves to show.

PSALM CXXVII.

God's Blessing Necessary to Prosperity.

EXCEPT God build the house,
  It will unbuilt remain;
Except the city God shall guard,
  The watchmen wake in vain.

In vain ye daily toil,
  And eat the bread of care;
God his beloved gives in sleep
  The wealth ye fain would share.

Children are gifts from God;
  Bless'd they who them receive!
As arrows in a warrior's hand,
  They power to parents give.

Whose quiver's full of them
  He has great cause for joy;
He never can be put to shame,
  But shall his foes destroy.

PSALM CXXVIII.
The Advantages of Piety.

HAPPY is he who fears the Lord,
  And walks in wisdom's ways;
The fruit he of his toil shall eat,
  And prosper all his days.

His cheerful wife within his house
  A fruitful vine shall be;
His children round his table sit,
  Like the spreading olive tree.

Behold! thus happy is the man
  Who doth God truly fear;
God out of Zion blesses him,
  And bends his prayer to hear.

He shall through all his days behold
  Zion's prosperity;
Yea, with long life he shall be blessed,
  And children's children see.

PSALM CXXIX.
Acknowledgment of God's Mercies.

NOW Israel may say,
  My foes have me assail'd,
From early youth until this hour;
  But they have not prevail'd.

The plowers plowed my back,
   And there long furrows made;
But God in my behalf appeared,
   And their designs forbade.

Let them who Zion hate
   Fall to their foes a prey!
Or be like grass on the house top,
   Which withers soon away.

Nor let the passers by
   Kind wish for them express;
Nor to them, as to others, say,
   "You may God greatly bless!"

PSALM CXXX.

Prayer for Forgiveness.

OUT of deep waters, O my God,
   To thee in prayer I cry!
My earnest supplication hear,
   Save me from evils nigh.

If thou didst treasure up our sins,
   Who could to thee draw near?
But now forgiveness is with thee,
   That we thy Name may fear.

Thou art my trust; guarded by thee,
   I should all danger scorn;

And now for thee longs more my soul,
    Than watchmen for the morn.

O Israel, trust in the Lord,
    Both merciful and just;
With him there full redemption is
    For all who in him trust.

PSALM CXXXI.

Humility and Contentment.

NOT haughty is my heart, O Lord,
    Nor lofty are mine eyes;
To naught too great or high for me
    Does my ambition rise.
Yea, I have now my mind composed,
    And quieted to rest;
So that my soul is like a child,
    Weaned from its mother's breast.
O Israel, trust in the Lord!
    For they who trust are blessed.

PSALM CXXXII.

Prayer at the Dedication of the Temple.

REMEMBER David, O my God,
    In his affliction sore!

How that he made a solemn vow,
  And to Jehovah swore:
"I will not go into my house,
  And quiet give my mind,
Nor even take repose in sleep,
  Till him a place I find."
We've heard or seen how that the ark
  Was moved from place to place;
But let us now before it come—
  Approach the throne of grace.

Arise into thy rest, O Lord,
  Thou and thy ark of power!
Be thy priests clothed with righteousness;
  Ye saints, the Lord adore!
O for thy servant David's sake
  Regard my earnest prayer;
Thou wilt not from thy words depart
  Which thou to him didst swear:
"I will his son a ruler make,
  His children, too, will own;
And if they keep my covenant
  Their's ever is the throne."

Zion God takes for his abode,
  (His words I gladly tell,)
"This is my chosen resting-place,
  Here I delight to dwell.

And I will her provisions bless,
  On her my mercies pour;
Salvation all her priests shall clothe,
  The saints my name adore.
The power of David I'll exalt,
  And light upon him shed;
I will his foes all clothe with shame,
  The crown shall deck his head."

PSALM CXXXIII.

Of Unity among Brethren.

HOW pleasant is the fellowship
  Of brethren in the Lord!
How good in unity to dwell,
  And in his praise accord!

'Tis like the rich anointing oil
  Which, poured on Aaron's head,
Ran down his beard, and sweet perfume
  O'er all his garments shed.

'Tis like the dew on Hermon falls,
  And sprinkles Zion o'er;
For here his blessing God commands,
  And life for evermore.

PSALM CXXXIV.

Praise offered to God in his Temple.

O PRAISE the Lord, all ye his saints,
   Who serve him night and day,
And in his temple lift your hands,
   And his commands obey:
And may the Lord, by whom we live,
From Zion his rich blessing give.

PSALM CXXXV.

Exhortation to Praise God.

PRAISE ye the Lord, his faithful saints,
   For he is good and kind;
Whom he has chosen for his own,
   To bless them is inclined.
Above all gods the Lord is great,
   And does his sov'reign will
In heaven, and earth, and in the sea;
   He doth all places fill!
He causes all the clouds that rise,
   The lightning and the rain;
And from his storehouse brings the wind,
   Which sweep o'er all the main.
He all of Egypt's first-born smote,
   And wonders great displayed;

He all the kings of Canaan slew,
    His people mighty made.
The land for their inheritance
    To Israel he gave,
And he will evermore endure,
    And all his people save.
He is the Judge of all the earth,
    And just are his commands;
But the idols of the nations are
    The work of human hands.
Their mouths speak not, nor have they
        breath;
    They neither see nor hear;
Their makers and their worshipers
    As vain as they appear.
Praise ye the Lord, his faithful saints,
    All ye the Lord who fear!
Yea, out of Zion praise the Lord!
    Praise ever let us hear!

PSALM CXXXVI.

A Psalm of Thanksgiving.

GIVE thanks to the Lord who is kind;
Sing praise to the God of all gods;
Thanks offer the Lord of all lords;
      Lives his goodness forever!

Praise Him who great wonders has done,
Whose wisdom the high heavens made,
And o'er waters extended the earth:
> Lives his goodness forever!

Adore Him who made the great lights,
The sun to have rule o'er the day,
And the moon and the stars o'er the night:
> Lives his goodness forever!

He smote all of Egypt's first-born,
And Israel brought from their midst,
With a hand strong and mighty to save:
> Lives his goodness forever!

He divided the sea into parts,
Made Israel pass through the midst,
And Pharaoh therein overthrew:
> Lives his goodness forever!

He us through the wilderness led,
Smote the kings of the land for our sake,
And slew mighty chiefs in our way:
> Lives his goodness forever!

Smote Sihon, the Amorites' king,
And Og, who in Bashan did reign,
And gave to his people their lands:
> Lives his goodness forever!

Yea, he a rich heritage gave
His servants while still on the earth;
Remembering their humble estate:
        Lives his goodness forever!

He us from our foes has redeemed;
He food to all people now gives:
O praise ye the great God above!
        Lives his goodness forever!

PSALM CXXXVII.

Jewish Captives in Babylon.

BY Babylon's streams we sat down,
    And wept when of Zion we thought;
And hanged on the willows around
    Our harps, in our sadness unsought.

Us to grieve, them our foes bade us string,
    And wake them to gladness and mirth;
But how Zion's songs shall we sing,
    Afar from the land of our birth?

If I love not Jerusalem yet,
    Or of her ever thoughtless become,
May my right hand its cunning forget,
    My tongue to its sweet strains be dumb!

Let Edom, who urged on our foes,
    And felt in our sorrows delight,
O Lord, soon awake from repose;
    Condemned and reproved in thy sight.

And Babylon, soon upon thee
    Shall thy cruel slaughters return;
Thy little ones slain thou shalt see,
    And evermore desolate mourn.

PSALM CXXXVIII.

The Goodness and Truth of God.

WITH my whole heart will I praise thee,
    And with thy saints rejoicing sing:
I in thy house will bow the knee
    Before my Saviour and my King.

Thy truth and goodness shall abide,
    Throughout the universe believed;
For thou thy word hast magnified,
    Done more than mortal had conceived.

My prayer thou hast been pleased to hear,
    And strength and comfort to me give;
Earth's mighty ones thy name shall fear,
    And joyful in thy service live.

God in the humble takes delight;
    The proud he at a distance sees;
He ever will protect the right,
    For him can nothing sinful please.

Us he will save by his right hand,
    And all his promises fulfill;
His goodness evermore shall stand,
    For changeless is Jehovah's will.

PSALM CXXXIX.

The Universal Presence and Knowledge of God.

O LORD, thou me hast searched and known!
Lie down, or rise, I'm not alone!
Thou art acquainted with my ways,
And ever on my thoughts dost gaze.
My words unspoken thou dost see;
Yea, all I am is known to thee;
On every side hedged is my way,
Thy hand thou dost upon me lay.
Such knowledge is too high for me,
I can't conceive how it can be.
Where shall I from thy presence go,
Where me thy Spirit shall not know?
Should I to highest heaven rise,
Thou, Lord, art there, for ever wise;

Or even into hell should dare,
Behold, th' Omniscient One is there!
Or the swift wings of morning take,
And o'er the sea my dwelling make,
Thy presence there thou wouldst reveal,
And thy right hand should guard me still:
Or should I in the darkness hide,
Light my vain effort would deride:
To thee, whose will all things obey,
Night shines as clearly as the day.

Thou didst to me existence give;
Yea, in my mother's womb me weave.
How wonderfully I am made!
I'm almost of myself afraid!
Too marvelous thy works to tell,
And this my soul now knows full well.
My substance was not hid from thee,
While yet unformed thou didst me see.
When I was curiously wrought,
I then received thy care and thought;
And ere my members were begun,
Thy book contained them every one.
How precious are thy thoughts to me;
They are, O God, a boundless sea!
Them I've no power to understand;
They would outnumber far the sand.

When I awake, I'm with thee still;
For thou the universe dost fill.

O that thou wouldst the wicked slay!
Ye men of blood, get ye away!
For they speak evil, Lord, of thee,
And proudly work iniquity.
Them that hate thee do I not hate?
Would I not haste their coming fate?
I count them all as my own foes,
For they thy righteous laws oppose.
Search me, O God, and know my heart,
And bid my evil thoughts depart!
Help me thy precepts to obey,
And lead me in the ancient way.

PSALM CXL.

Prayer for Aid against the Wicked.

DELIVER me from evil men
  Who practice violence;
They daily stir up war; their hearts
  Are full of vile intents:
Like serpents sharpen they their tongues;
  Poison their lips conceal—
Defend me from their cruelty;
  Thy saving hand reveal.

The proud for me have hidden snares,
　A net for me have spread;
But thou, Jehovah, art my God,
　My all-sufficient aid;
And when to battle I go forth
　Thou shelterest my head.
Grant not the wicked their desire;
　Do thou defeat their aim;
And let them not exalt themselves,
　But cover them with shame.
Let burning coals upon them fall,
　Cast them into the fire,
And into waters deep and wide,
　And thus let them expire.
The slanderer upon the earth
　Shall never strong become;
The violent shall wrath pursue—
　Destruction is their doom.
But thou th' afflicted dost regard;
　Thou their defense wilt be;
The righteous still shall praise thy name,
　And dwell secure with thee.

PSALM CXLI.

Prayer for Deliverance from Enemies.

MAKE haste to save me, O my God,
　For unto thee I cry;

Turn not away thy gracious ear,
 Do not my suit deny.
O let my prayer before thee come,
 As incense to thee rise;
And the uplifting of my hands,
 As th' evening sacrifice.
Let me not with the wicked join,
 Thy laws not disobey:
Set thou a watch before my mouth,
 And guard whate'er I say.
Let me be smitten by the just,
 It shall a kindness be;
Oil for my head is their reproof,
 It warns and strengthens me;
And though repeated, I would still
 Receive it gratefully.

Let not the wicked me assail,
 Against them now I pray;
Their judges hurl upon the rocks,
 That others may obey,
And kindly hear the peaceful words
 Which thou to them shalt say.
At the grave's mouth our bleaching bones
 Are scattered all around;
Like clods of earth, and chips of wood,
 They fairly strew the ground:

But to thee, Lord, I turn mine eyes,
  I put my trust in thee;
O let my life not be poured out,
  From snares of foes set free;
But may they to them fall a prey:
  Themselves the victims be.

PSALM CXLII.
Prayer in Distress.

UNTO the Lord I raise my voice,
  And my desires express;
Before him pour out my complaints,
  And set forth my distress.
When grief my spirit overwhelms,
  Thou watchest where I go;
But though I look around on earth,
  There me no man will know.
No man cares for me, refuge fails;
  O Lord, I cry to thee;
Thou art my refuge in distress,
  Thou wilt my portion be.
My persecutors now prevail;
  I am brought very low;
Do thou from prison bring me forth,
  And me thy favors show.
Then will the righteous me sustain,
  With me praise thee below.

PSALM CXLIII.

Prayer when Oppressed by Enemies.

O LORD, hear thou my earnest prayer
  While now I look to thee;
Thou ever just and faithful art—
  Wilt thou not answer me?
Do not in judgment on me sit,
  Nor my past life review;
For no man living would be found
  Before thee just and true.
I by my foes am smitten down,
  Brought to a wretched state;
My spirit is in me o'erwhelmed,
  My heart is desolate.
I think about the days of old,
  The labors of thy hand;
And then my soul thirsts after thee
  Like a parched, thirsty land.
O hear me, ere my spirit fails,
  Hide not thy face from me;
Lest I become like to the dead,
  Let me thy goodness see.
I trust in thee; to me make known
  The way that I should take,
While to thee I lift up my soul:
  Nor to my foes forsake.

In thee do I my refuge seek,
   Teach me to do thy will;
Let thy good Spirit in the path
   Of duty lead me still.
Revive me for thine own name's sake,
   And save me from distress;
In mercy all my foes cut off,
   And me, thy servant, bless.

PSALM CLXIV.

Thanksgiving and Intercession.

BLESSED be the Lord, my guide in war,
   And guard in danger's way;
He is my refuge and my shield—
   Gives nations to my sway.
Lord, what is man, or what his son,
   That thou shouldst for him care?
To a mere shadow passing by,
   We may his life compare.
O bow the heavens and come down,
   The mountains touch with flame;
Shoot thy fierce lightnings 'mid my foes,
   Make them revere thy name.
From the deep waters rescue me;
   Make me securely stand;
Save from the cruel, alien foe,
   For false in his right hand!

Then a new song to thee I'll sing,
    The psaltery employ;
For thou hast saved me from the sword,
    And filled my heart with joy.
Our sons like thrifty plants shall grow,
    And in the land abound;
Our daughters, too, like pillars fair,
    In palaces are found.
Our garners shall with fruits be filled;
    Our stock yield their increase;
And no disturbance shall there be,
    But quietness and peace.
How happy are the people found
    In such a prosp'rous state;
They have Jehovah for their God,
    Who makes them truly great.

PSALM CXLV.

PART I.

Praise the God of Nature.

THEE will I praise, eternal King,
And gladly in thy presence sing,
Come every day thy throne before,
And praise thy name for evermore.
Great is the Lord I know full well,
His greatness is unsearchable:

All nations shall thy works declare,
And find delight in praise and prayer.

I will thy majesty proclaim,
And speak the glories of thy name;
While stars upon me nightly beam,
Thy wondrous works shall be my theme.

And men, beholding on the earth
Thy deeds, shall gladly set them forth;
Shall join redeeming grace to praise,
And sing thy goodness all their days.

PART II.

Praise the God of Providence.

OUR God is good to all below,
In mercy rich, to anger slow;
His favors every-where prevail;
His tender mercies never fail.

Thy works, O Lord, thy praise proclaim;
Thy saints, rejoicing, bless thy name;
Thy subjects of thy kingdom speak,
And pleasure in thy service seek.

They would thy majesty make known,
That all may bow before thy throne:
Thy kingdom shall o'er earth extend,
And thy dominion never end.

Thou dost uphold them that would fall,
And hear their voice who on thee call;
Thou dost raise up those in distress,
And all thy creatures greatly bless.

PART III.

Praise the God of Grace.

ON thee, O God, the nations wait,
For in thy hand abides their fate;
Thou dost thy creatures duly feed,
And give to all as they have need.

Thou righteous art in all thy ways,
And ready to accept our praise;
Thou ever dost incline thine ear,
The earnest prayer of faith to hear.

To praying ones thou help dost give,
And every burdened heart relieve;
And guard thy saints in the dread hour,
When o'er the wicked death has power.

Now will I worship thee, my God;
My mouth shall sound thy praise abroad;
And let all men thy name adore,
And sing thy praise for evermore.

PSALM CXLVI.

The Justice and Mercy of God.

PRAISE ye the Lord, his saints on earth;
  My soul, his name adore:
Him will I serve while I have breath;
  I'll praise him evermore.

On him I ever will rely,
  Nor even princes trust;
In man alone there is no help;
  He soon returns to dust.

Happy is he whose help is God,
  By whom all things were made;
Who truth maintains for evermore,
  And grants th' oppressed his aid.

Unto the hungry he gives food,
  And sets the pris'ners free;
He raises them that are bowed down,
  And makes the blind to see.

He in the righteous takes delight;
  The stranger he defends;
The fatherless and widow guards,
  And blessings on them sends.

He to the wicked is opposed,
　And crooked makes their way;
In Zion he for ever reigns—
　O let us praise and pray!

PSALM CXLVII.

God's Goodness to his People.

'TIS good to praise the Lord our God;
　Such acts becoming are;
He builds up Zion on the earth,
　Gathers his saints from far.
He heals the broken heart, gives peace
　When grief the soul inflames;
He counts the number of the stars,
　And calls them by their names.
Only the God we serve is great,
　Th' Almighty One is he;
His understanding's infinite,
　His love a boundless sea.
The lowly he to power lifts up;
　Them his rich mercies crown;
He passes the proud unnoticed by,
　And hurls the wicked down.

Thanksgiving offer to the Lord,
　And praise his name again;

The heavens he covers o'er with clouds,
  And sends the gentle rain.
He causes grass on earth to grow,
  And gives the beasts their food;
He hears when the young ravens cry:
  He's to all creatures good.
In armies he takes no delight,
  Remembers they are dust;
But he takes pleasure in his saints
  Who in his mercy trust.

O Zion, praise thy God! Let all
  Their gratitude express!
He strengthens now thy bars and gates,
  And doth thy children bless.
In all thy borders he gives peace,
  And finest of the wheat;
Swift runs his word o'er all the earth,
  Naught can with it compete.
He scatters snow o'er all the ground,
  The hoar-frost by his hand;
His ice like morsels casts around:
  Who can his cold withstand?
He sends his word abroad again,
  And makes the wind to blow;
They melt before his wondrous power;
  And then the waters flow.

To Zion he his law has given,
  And made his mercies known;
With whom has he so kindly dealt?
  Let us the Giver own!

PSALM CXLVIII.

Invocation to all Things to Praise God.

PRAISE ye the Lord! From heaven praise,
  In the sublimest height;
Angelic hosts, and sun, and moon,
  And all ye stars of light!
Praise him, ye highest, brightest heavens!
  Ye waters in the sky!
Let all his works revere his name,
  And in his praises vie!
For by his word they all were made,
  His praises to express;
And to them all he gave his law,
  Which they cannot transgress.

Praise ye the Lord, all on the earth,
  And monsters of the deep!
Yea, praise him, fire, hail, vapor, snow,
  And winds his word that keep!
Mountains and hills, and spreading trees,
  Cattle, and creeping things,

Beasts of the wood, birds of the air,
   Ye people, and ye kings;
Rulers and ruled, young men and maids,
   Old men and children; all
Unite to praise Jehovah's name,
   His majesty extol!
For his name is exalted high,
   His glory, worlds above;
It power omnipotent displays,
   And unexampled love.
And power he to his people gives,
   And makes their glory known;
He takes them close unto himself,
   And claims them for his own.

PSALM CXLIX.

God Praised for Victories.

PRAISE ye the Lord, his worshipers,
   And to him raise your voice;
In God, who made him by his power,
   Let Israel rejoice.
Zion, be joyful in your King;
   In dance praise ye his name;
With harp and timbrel give him praise:
   He doth your service claim.
God pleasure in his people takes,
   And will their wants relieve;

Hence let them even on their beds
    Him joyful praises give.
Let them go forth to glorious war,
    To execute his will;
And make their land secure and strong,
    Who his commands fulfill.
For this is the announced decree
    Of Israel's just God,
His worship to preserve on earth:
    Hence shout his praise abroad!

PSALM CL.

Exhortation to Praise God.

PRAISE God in his sanctuary!
    Praise him in his glorious sky!
Praise him for his mighty deeds!
    Praise him who is great and high!

Praise him with the trumpet's sound!
    Praise with harp and psaltery!
Praise with timbrel and with dance!
    Praise with pipe's sweet minstrelsy!

Praise with all stringed instruments!
    Praise with cymbals clear and high!
Praise him all things that have breath!
    Praise the Lord of earth and sky!

INDEX.

Acknowledgment of God's Mercies ....Page 233
Admonition to keep God's Commandments 130
A Grateful Song of Praise 175
A Hymn in Time of Great Persecution.................. 136
A Hymn of Praise..................................... 100
A Light to our Path.................................. 219
A National Hymn of Praise 107
An Appeal to Wicked Rulers 141
An Exhortation to Praise God......................... 167
An Historic Sketch of the Sins of Israel 184
An Invective against the Wicked...................... 97
An Offering of Praise 47
Appeal to God against the Wicked 162
A Prayer in Sickness 66
A Psalm for the Sabbath Day 160
A Psalm of Praise 169
A Psalm of Praise 206
A Psalm of Thanksgiving 239
A Sacramental Hymn.................................. 197
Ascension of Christ................................... 89

Cast me not off with the Wicked 44
Chastisement for our Good 164
Christ our Refuge..................................... 102
Christ the Glorious King 77
Christ the Good Shepherd 38
Christ the Corner-Stone............................... 208

INDEX.

Comfort of God's People ....Page	49
Complaints concerning Enemies	226
Confession and Prayer of a Penitent...................	88
Confidence in Divine Protection	227
Confidence in God's Care.............................	95
Confidence in God's Mercy	17
Confidence in the Divine Protection...................	206
Confident Supplication	26
Constancy of the Righteous	215
David Pleads God's Covenant	155
Death the Fate of All	83
Deceitful Foes and Treacherous Friends	72
Delight in God's Law	214
Description of Christ's Crucifixion	36
Description of the Wicked............................	58
Descriptive of Christ's Kingdom......................	37
Desire to be with God's People	42
Evening Prayer	12
Exhortation to Join in Worship.......................	166
Exhortation to Praise God............................	238
Exhortation to Praise God............................	259
Exhortation to Praise the Ascended Saviour	81
Exultation in God's Goodness	193
Exultation in God's Goodness	229
Fervent Aspirations after God........................	103
Firm Trust in God...................................	165
God Blesses and Protects his People...................	53
God Cares for Man...................................	16
God Defends the Righteous...........................	61
God Faithful to his Word.............................	21
God his People's Defence	59

INDEX.

God in Nature and Grace ....Page	161
God our Creator, Governor, and Protector..............	51
God our Support in Persecution	115
God Praised for his Law.............................	225
God Praised for Victories............................	258
God Prospers the Righteous..........................	62
God Reigns over Nations.............................	162
God Speaking in his Sanctuary	85
God Sustains and Saves the Righteous................	62
God the Christian's Portion...........................	123
God Trusted in Danger...............................	98
God's Admonition to his People......................	189
God's Blessing Necessary to Prosperity	232
God's Covenant with David	154
God's Demand of his People	85
God's Demand of the Wicked.........................	87
God's Glory in his Works and Word..................	82
God's Glory seen in a Thunder-storm..................	45
God's Goodness to his People	255
God's Goodness to Men in Different Circumstances.......	189
God's Judgments Just................................	216
God's Law a Vast Deep	222
God's Law Just and True............................	222
God's Law makes Wise	219
God's Law our Happiness........	226
God's Mercy and Greatness Pleaded in Prayer	147
God's Works Display Himself........................	162
Grateful Praise and Adoration........................	171
Grief for Others' Disobedience.......................	224
Grief for the State of the Church.....................	128
Humility and Contentment...........................	235
Hymn for Social Worship............................	205
Intercession for a Ruler	84
Invective against Enemies............................	194

264 INDEX.

Invitation to Engage in Worship ....Page 170
Invocation to all Things to Praise God................ 257
Israel coming out of Egypt........................... 201
Israel compared to a Vine 137

Jewish Captives in Babylon........................... 241

Longing after God.................................... 73
Longing for God's Law................................ 223
Longing for God's Worship 143

Means of Moral Purity................................ 210
Morning Prayer 13

Of Unity among Brethren 237
On Trusting God when in Distress 204
Our Safety is in God 96

Perfection of God's Law.............................. 218
Persecution of the Righteous......................... 114
Piety Better than Wealth............................. 212
Pious Regard for God's Law 220
Praise after Victory................................. 207
Praise for National Independence 75
Praise for Victory 35
Praise Offered to God in his Temple 238
Praise the God of Grace.............................. 253
Praise the God of Nature............................. 251
Praise the God of Providence 252
Praise to the Supreme Ruler......... 168
Praise ye the Lord................................... 200
Prayer against Enemies 142
Prayer and Praise 92
Prayer and Trust..................................... 22
Prayer at Morning Worship 172

INDEX.

Prayer at the Dedication of the Temple..........Page	235
Prayer concerning False Witnesses.....................	56
Prayer concerning Public Crimes	57
Prayer concerning Secret Foes	55
Prayer for Aid against the Wicked....................	245
Prayer for a Revival..................................	145
Prayer for Assistance in Old Age......................	117
Prayer for Deliverance from Enemies...................	93
Prayer for Deliverance from Enemies	246
Prayer for Divine Aid.................................	211
Prayer for Divine Guidance............................	40
Prayer for Divine Mercy...............................	239
Prayer for Forgiveness	234
Prayer for Guidance and Protection....................	148
Prayer for Protection	104
Prayer for Protection from Enemies	15
Prayer for the Church in Persecution..................	124
Prayer for the Prosperity of Zion	174
Prayer in Distress....................................	14
Prayer in Distress	48
Prayer in Distress	248
Prayer in National Disaster	76
Prayer in National Distress	99
Prayer in Temptation	70
Prayer in Temptation	116
Prayer of One in Deep Distress........................	173
Prayer of Penitence...................................	63
Prayer when Oppressed by Enemies......................	249
Pray for the Peace of Zion	228
Prosperity of the Righteous...........................	199
Regal and Sacerdotal Powers of Christ.................	196
Rejoicing in Christ	43
Rejoicing in God's Goodness...........................	25
Religious Experience Told	108

INDEX.

Security of the Church..........................Page 79

Thanksgiving and Intercession........................ 250
Thanksgiving for Victory 127
The Advantages of Piety 233
The Authority of the Wicked Deprecated 18
The Beauty and Security of Zion 82
The Brevity of Human Life........................... 157
The Captive's Return................................ 231
The Church the Lamb's Bride......................... 78
The Confidence of the Righteous 11
The Courage of the Righteous........................ 211
The Deceitful Tongue................................ 89
The Deliverance of the Israelites................... 129
The Exile's Return 100
The Faithfulness and Mercy of God................... 151
The Glory of Zion 149
The God of Grace and Nature Praised 105
The God of Israel with his People 110
The Goodness and Truth of God 242
The Goodness of God to Israel traced in their History.... 180
The Immutability of God............................. 175
The Lord of Sabaoth in Action....................... 28
The Lord in Contrast with Idols..................... 202
The Justice and Mercy of God 254
The People who know the Joyful Sound................ 153
The Penitent Pardoned............................... 50
The Penitent Encouraged............................. 54
The Portion of the Wicked in this Life 121
The Prayer of One in Great Distress 150
The Righteous and the Wicked Contrasted   9
The Righteous Exhorted to Trust in God.............. 60
The Righteous greatly Blessed....................... 209
The Righteous Protected and Wicked Punished 20
The Reward of Charity............................... 71

The Safety of Him who Trusts in God ....Page	158
The Safety of Obedience.............................	213
The Sinner Saved....................................	67
The Triumphant Reign of Christ......................	119
The Universal Presence and Knowledge of God.........	243
The Use of Afflictions...............................	215
The Vanity of Human Life............................	65
The Value of a Place in God's House..................	144
The Wonderful and Manifold Works of God............	177
The Work of Redemption	68
Their Safety who Trust in God........................	230
Triumph of Christ over his Foes......................	10
Trust in God's Providence	217
Universal Depravity	22
Universal Depravity.................................	91
Waiting for God's Blessing	221
Who Will be Saved..................................	24

THE END.

www.ingramcontent.com/pod-product-compliance
Lightning Source LLC
Chambersburg PA
CBHW032138230426
43672CB00011B/2375